The 40 Day Experiment

Achieving Intimacy with God

Barbara Colacchia

ISBN 978-1-64416-560-7 (paperback)
ISBN 978-1-64416-561-4 (digital)

Christian Faith Publishing, Inc.
832 Park Avenue
Meadville, PA 16335
www.christianfaithpublishing.com

Printed in the United States of America

I dedicate this book to my husband Anthony and my daughters Angelina and Teresa; thank you for always encouraging me to seek God. I would like to also acknowledge my church family, especially Pastor Christopher W. Hussey, who I lovingly call my big bro, as well as Pastor Nataly Galichansky, and Pastor Troy Bramblet who mentor me, disciple me and always see the gold in me. A very special thank you also goes to, in no particular order, Debbie Castner, George and Renay Zamloot, Shelley Bossart, Judy Folkerts, Nancy Dalrymple, John and Kristina Berenzy, and Barbara Labrie, who have committed themselves to intercede for me and my family as I continue to pursue God and seek His kingdom. I love you all.

Preface

No one is ever so far gone into a life of sin that God cannot redeem them. Likewise, no one is ever so intimate with God that there isn't room for more intimacy. There is always more! The intent of this book is to bring many into the kingdom of God as well as leading those that are already in Christ into a deeper, more meaningful, intimate relation with Jesus Christ our Savior. If you have not accepted Jesus Christ as Savior I encourage you to repent of your sin and acknowledge you are in need of a Savior. Salvation involves a combination of two things, faith, faith that Jesus is the son of God and died for your sin. It is a gift of grace, we cannot earn our salvation. Repentance is the second thing. Repentance is not just being sorry for your sins but turning from your sin. To take it one step further, it is asking God to give you His eyes for those sins so that you see them the way God does. Accepting Jesus Christ as Savior is having Him as Lord of your life and it is a decision that will forever change the rest of your life. Salvation is not about getting to heaven only; it is that and so much more. It is power, grace, and mercy given to you through the Holy Spirit to trample the enemy under your feet as the Holy Spirit indwells you every day of your life.

If you have come to that point where sin and the ways of the world have overwhelmed you and you know you need a Savior and are willing to repent, confess with your lips and believe in your heart that Jesus Christ is Savior, then I invite you to pray this prayer:

> Dear God in heaven, I come to you in the
> name of Jesus. I confess that I am a sinner, and I

am sorry for my sins and the life that I have lived; I need your forgiveness.

I believe that Your only begotten Son Jesus Christ, shed His precious blood on the cross at Calvary and died for my sins, and I am now willing to turn from my sin.

I confess and repent of all my sins, known and unknown.

You said in Romans 10:9 that if we confess Jesus as Lord and believe in our hearts that God raised Jesus from the dead, we shall be saved.

Right now, I confess Jesus as the Lord of my life. In my heart I believe that God raised Jesus from the dead. This very moment I accept Jesus Christ as my own personal Savior, and according to His Word, right now I am saved.

Thank you, Jesus, for Your unlimited grace which has saved me from my sins. Therefore, Lord Jesus, transform my life so that I may bring glory and honor to you alone and not to myself.

Thank you, Jesus, for dying for me and giving me eternal life. *Amen.*

Congratulations, now get yourself to a good Bible-believing church and invest in a Bible.

Those of you who have already committed your life to Christ, this book is for you also. God requires of us two things, faith and love. Without faith it is impossible to please God. We are to love God with all our heart, soul, and mind and love our neighbor as we love ourselves. Faith and love may only be two things, but if we are honest with ourselves, we will admit that it is easier said than done; that is, unless we have intimacy with Christ through the Holy Spirit.

Communion and union with Christ is what we were born for. Yet somehow, I had convinced myself that I could only get to a certain level of intimacy and that was it. The higher levels of communion were set aside for other people; you know, those real pious ones, or just pastors or just…That was a lie I believed. We, as believers, are disciples of Jesus. As disciples we are to imitate Jesus. Jesus demonstrated what it looked like as a man to walk in constant communion with the Father. This means that it is available to us, all of us, no matter who we are. God wants to draw near to us, but we need to do our part and draw near to Him. This book demonstrates how faithful God is. Intimacy, deep intimacy, is available to everyone. At first it may seem difficult or even impossible, but the truth is that it is a tactic of the enemy to convince us that we cannot have what God died to give us, that is, relationship and constant communion and union with Jesus Christ, the Holy Spirit, and God the Father. It is all available to us. It is a treasure that has been given to us through salvation that is to be fully utilized in this lifetime.

Introduction

*E*ncouraged by Frank Laubach's *Practicing His Presence: One of the Greatest Pieces of Christian Literature of all Time*, I've decided to keep a forty-day journal of what would happen if I took every thought captive to the obedience of Christ. I chose forty days because I am also doing a forty-day fast. It is not a Daniel fast but a fast nonetheless. I spent days wondering what I should fast from. Should I fast from all sugar? Should I just eat veggies? Should it be a complete Daniel fast? I asked the Lord and was convinced I had heard to fast from media. I had made my decision, no more social media for me. I am not one that posts a lot, however, I do find it to be mindless entertainment that helps me escape mentally. I thought it was a good idea after all; the time I spend scrolling through posts could be better spent scrolling through Scripture. Then I heard that still small voice saying, "Cookies and chocolate."

I thought, *Really?* Then I heard, "Fasting is so that the flesh will crave and you would hunger for Me." Okay, cookies and chocolate it is; apparently, I had not noticed that I had gotten into the habit of having a piece of chocolate or a cookie after every meal. I tell you what I was fasting from so that you would know that it's not so much about what you fast but it is about obedience.

Many whom I have spoken to during evangelistic opportunities have shared with me that it takes too much work to keep a relationship with God, too many rules to follow. Some say, "I'm too busy and don't have the time."

Others have told me that God would not want to waste His time with them. Some have even gone so far as to say that they are just fine and God should spend time with others that need Him more. The one thing I have heard the most is, "I can't have that kind of intense, intimate relationship with God. I'm not like so and so, I'm not holy enough, I'm not good enough, etc."

These people compare themselves to the pastors we see on TV or YouTube and say, "Well I'm not there yet."

This book will change that thinking. Up until now, you have been believing a lie. Draw near to God and He will draw near to you; it is His promise. James 4:7–8 puts it this way, "Submit therefore to God. Resist the devil and he will flee from you. Draw near to God and He will draw near to you. Cleanse your hands, you sinners; and purify your hearts, you double-minded."

In other words, it is a promise with a premise. We have to do our part and take our thoughts captive; that is one way of resisting the devil. Then we draw near to God, and while we draw near to God, He will bring things to memory that we may need to repent of or people we may need to forgive. When God does this, then in obedience and faith we are to repent and forgive.

If you have been desiring a deeper, more intimate relationship with God, this book is for you. Can a wife, homemaker, minister of the Gospel, seminary student working on a master's, and mother of two teenage girls who has some health issues take every thought captive and put it on Jesus for forty days? Well, my guess would be no, but I will try. The reason why I am performing this experiment is not to test God but to prove God's righteousness and kindness and to bring Him glory. The Scripture states to do everything to the glory of God.

Whether, then, you eat or drink or whatever
you do, do all to the glory of God. (1 Cor. 10:31)

Accordingly, if I seek first the kingdom of God, I do not have to worry about my life. God will provide what I need. Matt. 6:33 states, "But seek first His kingdom and His righteousness, and all these things will be added to you."

What are "all these things"? They are everything you can possibly need, emotional needs, physical needs, and spiritual needs.

Therefore, this experiment is to prove that although I may not be able to keep my mind on the kingdom, God, Jesus, and the Holy Spirit 24/7, I will prove that God is faithful to His word. He knows the heart and if we delight ourselves in Him, He will give us the desires of our hearts (Ps. 37:4–6). I am convinced that God will show Himself in ways I have never before seen. I know I will be used mightily by God for the kingdom, and I know that I will experience His presence like never before. How do I know this? He is a good, good Father, and I, His daughter, am asking for very specific things through this fast and giving all my body, mind, and soul has into keeping my eyes on the kingdom 24/7.

Well, here we go…

Day 1

*D*ay one started with a sense of expectation. I host a small group every other Wednesday, and the Lord had told me something powerful was about to happen. The meeting had gone wonderfully. As we worshipped, the presence of God was tangible. My friend, her name is Barb as well, taught on prophecy. Afterward, she prayed and imparted to us and asked us each to give a prophetic word to the person to our left. Most in the group had never given a prophetic word before. It was a powerful moment as prophetic words were given, some only a few words long but tears were streaming as God's word pierced these women in the heart and they all got to experience firsthand how intimately God knows them.

Then, my husband came home from work, which would not have been an issue if it weren't that he was home six hours earlier than usual. He had to leave work due to extreme pain in the abdomen. The doctor had told him she believed it was gallstones; our doctor is a wonderful woman of God. She's the only doctor I know of who will pray during a visit and ask God's presence into the room, a truly remarkable lady. Anyway, after prayer, he felt better. The ladies in the home group and I also prayed for him and then there was another measure of relief.

God's peace was so tangible, it was as if I could walk right through it. This is really important; you see, my husband is an auto mechanic and sometimes when the dealership gets slow, he loses his job. This has happened many times over the years. Seeing Tony home early meant he was now unemployed. I have not worked since I had a mini-stroke in 2011 which left me with basilar migraines that mimic strokes. Unemployment will not be a good thing. Yet, when he walked through the door, my first thought was, *"Hmmm, hope he is okay.*

My second thought which usually was my first was, *Oh, I hope he still has a job."* This thought made me feel scared. I mentally searched for a verse that I could take this thought captive with. The first verse that came to mind was, "For God has not given us the spirit of fear; but of power, and of love, and of a sound mind" (2 Tim 1:7). Taking the thoughts I had of fear captive to a promise of God allowed me to realize there was nothing to fear.

I drew near to God and instantly He drew near to me by giving me another Bible verse. God knew what was coming next and He prepared me. The verse was, 1 Jn. 4:18 "There is no fear in love; but perfect love casts out fear, because fear involves punishment, and the one who fears is not perfected in love." As thoughts of His perfect love washed over me a sense of God's presence filled the room.

Peace hit me like never before. My husband, Tony, then went on to tell me that he may need surgery and needs to get an ultrasound. My first reaction, if I were to go by my previous track record, would have been, "How are we going to pay for this or that?"; but it wasn't. It was wonderful. The whole day was full of different events where the still small voice directed me in a variety of ways like never before even in what to make for dinner, all while being completely covered in His peace. God did indeed give me the peace that surpassed all understanding, and it was wonderful!

Day 2

Today Tony has to go for his ultrasound; however, there is a blizzard-like condition outside. Yet, God's amazing peace still has me wrapped up in a blanket, and I am not concerned about going out on the slick roads.

Something else pretty amazing happened today. Let's just say that my husband was a little less nicer than I would have liked this morning. It seemed like he was trying to intentionally upset me, but things that would have normally made me blow my top did not. I will admit, I got close but before I blurted out something, a verse from a praise song would come out. I know that was God's doing.

So far, I am only a few hours into my day and I must admit I am not even close to taking every thought captive. This morning's incident proved that I can barely give a full thought completely to Jesus. We are fine on our own, but when someone else is in the mix like a husband, things can become challenging. However, as Frank Laubach once wrote, it is about the will. Today I choose to bend my will, die to self and say, "God this is what I think is right and want to do but you know best, lead me."

Throughout today God has given me an incredible grace to absorb negative words and hurtful actions and has enabled me with the ability to give it right to God and find joy in the situation. This is something that I have struggled with for many years, yet today, I realized that the more I am hurt by someone, the more it pushes me toward Jesus. This is a great revelation; there is no downside to the situation. If I am not emotionally hurt, great; but if I am, that's great too because I will get to experience the comfort of the Holy Spirit!

The day came to an end but not without its challenges. It is so easy to take my eyes off God. One moment I am in my office worshipping and doing school work and my desk and books are blessed with oil from heaven as I find myself wiping my desk and books several times. An hour later, I find myself being easily annoyed and feeling the tension of the day. However, I did notice something that took me by surprise. Usually, while spending family time together watching television, I find myself scrolling through social media; it's almost dare I say an addiction. Yet, not once did I even have a desire to look at my phone. During the commercials, my mind no longer went to thinking, *I wonder what kind of weird information can I find on Uber Facts?* but rather my thoughts went right to the Throne Room of God. This I also know was a grace from God. Things that would have normally upset me did not as I mentioned before. This changed the atmosphere at home. When you are focused on God, there is a "vibe" that comes off you that is contagious. I was emanating so much of the Holy Spirit in me that my children were catching it. There was an overwhelming joy that resonated through the house. Intimacy with God can sometimes be as simple as just feeling His presence and acknowledging He is there with a simple, "Thank you God."

Day 3

Yesterday's victories did not come without its defeats. Several times I was awakened by audible voices in my dream screaming obscenities. This has never happened before, so I will assume it was a demonic attack. Using one of Frank Laubach's letters as inspiration, I decided to do what I call the "one-minute test." In one of Mr. Laubach's letters, he challenges the reader to take one second out of every minute and give it to God. I decided to take this challenge, but with a slight modification. I chose to purposely pick one hour out of the day where I would set the timer for one minute over and over again for the duration of an hour. In other words for the sixty minutes that were in that hour, every sixty seconds, one second per minute would be devoted to God, thus the name, "one-minute test." I chose to do it between 12:00 p.m. and 1:00 p.m. I chose this time because it was not time dedicated to my studies or worship but regular time for a lack of a better word. It would be the time used to make lunch, do dishes, sweep, and hang out with my kids while they ate—you get the idea. The timer sounded every sixty seconds. When it went off the first few times, I would take a moment to praise God and celebrate His goodness; this would take a minute or two. When I was done, I would set the timer again and go about my business. After the timer went off a few more times, I changed from praise to reciting and thanking God for His promises. Everything seemed to be going smoothly and it was fun, but then the timer went off again and I found myself struggling to remember God's promises. The last fifteen minutes of the hour felt a lot longer than fifteen minutes.

In this process, I found out two things. One, I spend more time thinking about God than I had realized; when waiting for the timer to go off, I found myself singing praise songs or praying in the Spirit. The second thing I realized was that I did not know His word as well as I thought I did. When the timer rang toward the end of that hour, I blanked out and my two-minute prayers dwindled to one-second prayers where all I could say was the name Jesus. That is okay, but it was an eye-opener because in struggling to recall His promises, I realized there is probably so much more of God I have forgotten and so much more I don't even know.

It is a challenge of the will, my will. I must resolve not to be content with where I am. It is now 1:30 p.m. and although I will no longer be walking around with a timer, I will make a conscious effort to purposely put my thoughts on Jesus at least for one second out of every minute. Wanting to purposely spend more time with God, I decided to worship. My hopes are that at the very least I spend more time keeping my eyes on the kingdom today than I did an hour ago and that will increase with each hour passing until I die.

During my worship time, I looked at a map of the world and asked God to confirm if I was supposed to go to the nations, and during the "one-minute test," I claimed the promise in Psalms 2:8, "Ask me, and I will make the nations your inheritance, the ends of the earth your possession."

Within the hour, a friend comes for a visit and says, "The Lord told me I should really get you this."

It was a cup with a world map on it and inscribed on it was my name and inscribed on the other side is, "I know the plans I have for you…" Wow, talk about answered prayer. I felt as if God himself was saying, "Yes already, enough proof?"

This same friend asked if I would pray for her hand—she has a "trigger finger" that locks and is very painful. After praying, she noticed that a substantial amount of pain was gone and she could move her finger just a bit more; it was very stiff before we prayed and if it did bend, eventually it would stay bent. However, she screamed and said, "Oh wow, my other hand is healed!"

It turns out that she could not even make a fist with the other hand, yet God healed that hand completely! That hand too had a trigger finger that would lock, and praise God, it no longer locks; she was able to make a full fist multiple times and there is zero pain, hallelujah! My faith began to rise. God not only answered my question about an upcoming ministry trip but heard my prayers and healed my friend. If there was any doubt in me that God heard and answered my prayers it was now permanently gone.

Day 4

*A*s blissful as yesterday's day was, that evening became a much more difficult night. It turns out my husband did not show any gallstones in the ultrasound. Either God healed him of it (that's my guess) or he never had them; regardless, what did show up was an enlarged spleen. The spleen issue can be indicative of another problem; what it is, we don't know yet. I had never felt such a spiritual fight in my life to keep my peace, probably because I was never so aware of the peacemaker. I'm not going to lie, it took several text messages from a good friend and much bending of my own will and rebuking the enemy's voice to put my eyes back on Jesus. Even then, peace came but not like I had known it a few hours earlier.

I have to deal with the reality of the unknown and wait for Tony to decide to do blood work to know what we are dealing with. Today is going to be a great day of practicing His presence! I will attempt to do the "one-minute test," again.

It has been a long day. Most of my thoughts have come from fear or anger. All I can say for now is that it is much easier to focus on God when there is no one around, which really translates into: I have allowed the enemy an open door to come in and buffet me by agreeing with frustration, which comes from control, which ultimately comes from fear. Therefore, I have some repenting to do tonight. Yet, I focused more times on God today than yesterday. When I realized that the peace and joy I had been feeling was no longer there I knew it was time to renew my mind. How did I know this? Simple, because happiness comes through external things, but joy is internal. My joy is based on what my Savior Jesus Christ has done for me and no one nor nothing can take that away from me. If my joy level is low then I know I have given authority to Satan to take it away. I get that authority back by renewing my mind with Scripture and believing God's truth verses facts. These were the three verses that I recited over and over again today every time I did not feel God's peace. "The Lord is my helper, The Lord is the Sustainer of my soul" (Ps. 54:4). "I will give thanks to you O'Lord for it is good (Ps 54:6) and "Cast your burdens upon the Lord and He Will sustain you. He will never let the righteous to be shaken! (Ps. 55:22). It was through the reciting of Scripture that I was able to get back to that place of feeling God's presence around me. It is not a state of mind, it is the Holy's Spirit's physical appearance that He allows us to feel. The Holy Spirit is a person. In Scripture the Holy Spirit is referred to as "Him", the Holy Spirit can be grieved just as a person (Eph.4:30), lied to (Acts 5:3), obeyed (Acts 10:19–21) and honored just like a person. It was not that the Holy Spirit had left me, He will never leave me or forsake me, rather, I had allowed negative thoughts to consume me. These negative thoughts pulled my attention away from Jesus. Once my mind was renewed I was able to focus on Jesus again which brought about intimacy; knowing and remembering He loves and died for me.

So, I will count today a success. Tomorrow will be another opportunity to practice being in God's presence 24/7. I look forward to the next "one-minute test." I pray that tomorrow will be better than today in that I will take my thoughts captive to the obedience of God and focus on Him more tomorrow than I did today. I look forward to having my eyes opened to the many glorious things God does that I probably have been missing all along.

Day 5

*I*n order to focus more on God throughout my day, I've decided to incorporate a different tool today. Since I am enrolled in a master's program in seminary, I read a lot. Although what I am reading is God-centered, I am not necessarily focusing on God. Today I will try something new. As I read, in order to keep my eyes focused on the kingdom, at the start of every new page, I will pause and reflect on Jesus. I read slowly to begin with, and now it will take even longer to finish a chapter, but I believe the fruit will be worth it.

Today I realized that the prayers I pray, although they may be from victory and not to victory, were prayers just for me. What I mean by "from victory not to victory" is that I am not pleading with God for His goodness, rather I am declaring Scripture and God's promises knowing my prayer will be answered with a yes and amen. I realized that, I was praying prayers that would benefit just me and the things that concern me, not necessarily prayers that would benefit the body. There is nothing wrong with praying the prayers you need for yourself. However, we are part of something much bigger than ourselves, bigger than our families, and even bigger than our church. We are part of the universal church; we are a brother or a sister to every single person in the kingdom of God, wow!

As I was praying a "me" kind of prayer, the Lord asked me to pray for the church body (in this case, it was just for the body of the church I was physically in at the moment). As I started to do that, I felt the presence of God and I could barely stand; the more I prayed, the heavier the weight got until I was driven to my knees. I could feel Him so close to me—every muscle in my face was twitching uncontrollably. Later, I was keenly listening to the sermon, but I could not help but be aware of the Holy Spirit next to me. It was as if I could feel Him holding my hand. I had never felt so relaxed nor so energized all at the same time. I had so much joy, I could hardly sit still. I probably had a goofy expression on my face because all I wanted to do was laugh as the joy of the Lord filled me, but I was trying to hold it in because I wanted to be respectful, after all, I didn't want the pastor to think I was laughing at him. But then again if he saw my face and did notice the goofy expression, then he probably knew I was just enjoying Papa's embrace.

God is a rewarder of those who seek Him, it's true. This same morning my pastor asked me how I was doing; I thought I was fine, but what came out was a list of issues. We both laughed because it caught us both off guard, but God didn't condemn me or say, "Hey, is this how you practice my presence?"

God knows I've been drawing near to Him even though there may be moments of failure. Yet, after that mini-meltdown, God still allowed me to feel His beautiful presence and lifted those burdens right off me. I must admit I had to repent for not trusting that God has the situation in His control and for trying to control it myself. God is good.

If in case you were wondering the reward I seek from the rewarder is God Himself, God is the ultimate reward.

It was very exciting to realize that God was speaking to me continuously, perhaps I didn't hear it continuously, but when I did, it was amazing. I was given mental pictures, feelings, or words of what was going to happen next in my day seconds before it actually happened. It is as if all the spiritual gifts are being sharpened. If hearing His voice with this accuracy and consistency is the only thing that comes out of this experiment, I could be completely happy for the rest of my life. God, however, does not want us to settle for anything less than everything He has to offer. Besides, it's only day 5; I can't imagine what else Papa has in store for me.

I pray that this morning will not be an indicator of how the rest of the day will go. How easy it is to take my eyes off God for just a second and find I am walking in the filth that is my flesh. This morning I found cuss words, which by the way I have not used in years, come out of my mouth and for no reason at all. I was shocked at what came out of my mouth, not because what I said was all that bad according to the world's standard but because of the way it came out. This is good. This is God telling me there is something in me (of the many things) that needs work. I praise God for repentance and His faithfulness to love and teach us despite our rebellion and ignorance.

For the past day or two, when I read I have been pausing at the start of each new page and putting my eyes on the kingdom. However, I found myself yearning to praise Him before I got to the next page. Today I will slightly modify this tool by pausing after every paragraph and praising or thanking Jesus, maybe saying a prayer or perhaps just praying in the Spirit. I don't think it matters how long I do it for as long as it's done out of a joyful heart and not out of routine or rule. I am not doing this in order to bring legalism into my day but rather to train myself to be aware of Him as much as humanly possible. Even Timothy tells us to train ourselves in godliness.

Have nothing to do with godless myths and
old wives' tales; rather, train yourself to be godly.

> For physical training is of some value, but god-
> liness has value for all things, holding promise
> for both the present life and the life to come. (1
> Tim. 4:7–8).

As the day progressed, I was praising more than I had been the day before. I was watching TV and to myself, I was praising and thanking God for things when I paused and thought to myself I should stop what I was doing and praise for a minute. Ironically, I was already doing it.

I had the desire to do something I had not done in a while. A few years back, I had gotten into the habit of praying in the spirit and only in the spirit for a minimum of an hour at a time, but I haven't done so in a while. Today I had that desire and I was praying when the Lord said open your eyes and look. So I did; as I paced back and forth in my little office, I looked down and there it was—a drop of something on the floor had left a mark. Then I looked again and saw more, a trail of about nine tiny drops. You may think, who notices a drop, right? Well, two weeks ago my home office was renovated. The floors were newly painted gray; my office is in the basement and it's the only nice room the basement has. I sweep it every day and I know every single area of the floor. I took a good look at it when the furniture was moved back into the room and the newly painted floor chipped in several places. No one eats or drinks in there or anywhere in the basement for that matter, so you could imagine my surprise when I saw drops of something stained the floor. I asked my kids and they did not bring anything down, and I had no reason not to believe them as they had never done it before.

As I was staring at these drops wondering where they came from, I remembered the prayer I had prayed just a few days ago. That was the day I worshipped in front of my daughter, and that was a breakthrough for me. As I was worshipping, I had asked God to manifest himself in me. I specifically asked that I would be so satu-rated with His presence that I would leave a trail of oil everywhere I stepped. Yes, I know, it's an extreme request but that is what happens when you passionately pray—stuff just comes out of your mouth you wouldn't otherwise say. I believe this happens because on some level you let go of your thinking and are speaking the deepest desires of your heart you never dare share for fear someone may think you're nuts.

The spots on the floor caught me by surprise, but it really should not have; after all, I am a daughter who asked her Papa for a special gift. My Papa is a generous Father to all His children and a rewarder of those who seek Him. I didn't do anything to deserve it, but God still graced me with His presence. He graced me with drops of oil on the floor.

It is not about the physical manifestations although they are nice; it is all about the one who gives them. Did you ever stop and think why He gives them? Perhaps it's to display His glory, or perhaps it is just simply to let me know He is there. I can't control the manifestations, and this is not something that happens every day. However, I personally believe that because this book is to demonstrate His glory, faithfulness, and goodness, I will be seeing more of His manifestations. I will celebrate Him for all of them, big or small, and I will celebrate Him even if no manifestations occur. You don't love your earthly dad because of what he can give you, but you love him just because he's your dad. The same is true for God, but more so. God has already given me the biggest gift, salvation: freedom from an eternity in damnation and His power and authority to fulfill my days here on earth. I have a reason to celebrate Him.

This morning I started the day with anger and cussing. Yes, I repented but the damage was done, unkind words were spoken and I hurt my daughter's feelings. There were better ways I could have handled the situation and I was very disappointed in myself, but God was not; I had repented, He forgave and forgot that sin. In fact, God still drew near to me and surprised me with oil manifestations. This small gesture of oil from God overwhelmed me. God did not pull away from me because I spoke inappropriately. God will never leave me or forsake me. Although I know this, it brought me to a whole new level of intimacy with God. I experienced His promise of never leaving me today. It is probably not the first time it has happened but it is the first time I have noticed it. I am now actively looking for the ways God is manifesting Himself in my life throughout these forty days and in doing so I am trusting God more. This sounds funny to say but if we are honest with ourselves how many of us do not pray because we are afraid that the answer may be something we do not want to hear? I do not have that fear anymore. I know I can trust God because He loves me and He is the only one in the whole universe who wants what is best for me all the time.

*S*ometimes when something starts to consistently happen, you begin to think it is the way it is going to be from now on. The voice of God is an example. The past few days I have heard God speak to me as clearly as I would hear you speak to me if you were sitting next to me. This morning things were a little different. Since this experiment, I have not even looked at social media for no other reason than the desire has simply gone away. This morning I went on for a second just to check on a response from someone. I signed in to my account and quickly browsed through the notifications; I did not find what I was looking for so I quickly signed out. I had the urge to scroll through, but in my own thinking, I thought, *Nope, don't need to; I'm focusing on God.*

I had that urge again to scroll through the posts a couple of times before I realized it could be God telling me to do so. But could it be, after all it didn't come in the way I had been hearing Him all this week? God is faithful, and He hasn't left me just because I wasn't feeling Him or hearing Him the way I thought I should. I logged back on and thought to myself, *But why? I don't want to read about anyone's drama.*

Before I could have my next thought, which by the way was negative and not of God, I felt His gentle voice say, "So you could pray for them." Would you believe that the first post I saw was from someone who had just lost her father and had posted his biography and a loving testimony to his life? Through the post, you could feel the peace she had because he was now in heaven but also the pain one feels when grieving the loss of a father. After taking a moment and lifting her in prayer, I knew it was now okay to log out. I had done what Papa had wanted me to do.

The rest of the day was quiet and peaceful. One thing that was different was that late in the afternoon I had the urge to go into the "secret place". The secret place is what I call the place I go to where my focus is only God. It is where I pray and listen to His word uninterrupted. It can be a physical place like my office or the secret place can also be carried with you. It is a frame of mind where you have determined nothing will interrupt your time with God. Today I earnestly contended for certain things I've been praying a while for. I cannot remember the last time I prayed so earnestly. I think for the very first time my heart connected with all my words in praise. Let me explain. In worship, it is not unusual to praise God and so I do. I praise Him for what I know He has done and I praise Him in faith in the confident hope that He will honor my petition. Yet, I've always felt as if there was some sort of disconnect. There was an understanding that was missing on my part, a connection I felt I was missing. I just didn't know what it was and how to fix it. Today was different. When I praised God, I no longer praised Him in with generic words such as saying, "You are mighty; You are great." He is, but how is that specific to me, specific enough to make a heart connection?

Oftentimes, I praise God for things that are personal, for example, I praise you, God, that I could pay the mortgage today. I praise You, God, my husband arrived safely from work. I guess, what I am trying to say is that I never combined His majesty with the things I was praising Him for; it was either one or the other. However, today when I praise, I am praising Him because He is bigger than any demonic entity that could invade my home or has in the past. I praise Him because He is a God that does not require appeasing; His only requirement is faith and love, things we are naturally programmed to give. It is very difficult to express in words the freedom and the release that came from my innermost being when I was able to connect how God's majesty related to me in a personal way. It was wonderful.

God pulled me into a new level of intimacy today. It felt as if my heart connected with God's as I praised and thanked Him for His mercies and grace. There was a feeling of safety and security that I had never experienced before as I focused on God's majesty and how it pertained to me personally. It was a paradox, the more I focused my admiration on to God the more loved I felt by Him. As I concentrated on God's attributes, His kindness, His gentleness, His majestic ways, the more I realized that these are things that God wants to lavish me with and you. It is an endless cycle of beautiful love. The more I worship and praise Him, the more I feel His love for me. I do not know how else to explain it. Eventually, Satan tried to whisper one of His lies to me and told me it is all in my imagination. At this point, I took that thought captive. I asked God the following question, "Father, what lie am I believing?" Then God spoke to me and revealed the lie I had believed from the devil. I rebuked it and then replaced it with Scripture. In my case, I believed for a brief moment that what I was feeling was my imagination, it was not real. The Scripture I used to take that thought captive was 1 Jn. 2:27 "As for you, the anointing which you received from Him abides in you, and you have no need for anyone to teach you; but as His anointing teaches you about all things, and is true and is not a lie, and just as it has taught you, you abide in Him." God was teaching me about His love for me and about His attributes today. I can trust that what I was experiencing was real because He abides in me through the Holy Spirit.

One full week has passed since I've started this forty-day experiment; the following are some other blessings that occurred during the course of the week that were not journaled.

- During blizzard-like conditions, I no longer hated snow and the cold but found myself worshipping God and thanking him for a vehicle that could handle this type of weather. As I was thanking God for His goodness, a supernatural heat appeared on the back of my neck that made the remainder of my outing a pleasure.

- When incurring extra expenses due to a recent diagnosis, I realized there was no anger in me. In the past I would have been mad because it probably could have been prevented and because the funds had to come out of the savings which were being saved for something else. Yet, as I started to tell my daughter the prices of things, the next thing out of my mouth, which surprised me most of all, was, "Well, I'm not telling you this to complain or to bring any sort of guilt on anyone; I just want to glorify God and tell you how good God is. Isn't it good that we had the money to spend on this, isn't it good... that God is our provider and He will never leave us or forsake us? It even astonished me.

- When little things that normally would have aggravated me happened, my response was like never before. I would feel myself bubbling up ready to say something that I probably should not have, but instead I found myself smiling from ear to ear, blessing God for the thing that happened, not the negative thing, but for the outcome that will come from it. It is as if I am living in a Holy Spirit bubble looking at things through the rose-colored glass, except it is not glasses that are doing this, rather it is the reality that I now have chosen to live in and can by the grace of our Lord and savior Jesus Christ.

- The time I spend in worship has more than doubled; it can sometimes go on for well over an hour. This is a big thing to me; you see, I am from the camp that thinks time spent can't come back. If I spend time on one thing, then I have taken time away from something else that has to get done. However, the more time I spend in worship, the longer (in a good way) the day gets. I have done all I need to do with time to spare; it is simply incredible.

- I become very shy when worshipping in a small group, even more shy as the group becomes just one or two people, and if it is in front of my family, well I am extremely reserved, I feel judged. I usually ask them to go away if I am worshipping and they walk in. Well, on January 5, 2018, God delivered me of that. I was in my home office and was finishing up and about to leave when my oldest daughter walked in. I asked her if she wanted me to put on the worship music before I left, and she said, "Sure, pick what you want." I don't even remember what song was playing but the second the first note came on the air, the presence of the Lord fell. For an hour we worshipped the Lord together. I was singing at the top of my lungs (for those of you who know me, well you know I don't do that), I was dancing, and I was praising and declaring! It was amazing. His presence was so thick we could barely stand, so I lay on my face, again all things I would not do in front of someone especially my daughter; why, who knows? But today I was free of that. I worshipped as hard as I could with pure joy, and I didn't care who was there; in fact, I forgot she was there—it was heavenly!

- Words of knowledge are flowing like never before, not to mention His prompting in every area of my life. It is as if He is just talking to me for no reason other than to hang out with me. I was having breakfast and I felt God say to call the pharmacy and ask about the prescription; considering there were so many things He had said in the last three days that were spot on, there was no reason to ignore this prompting. I called the pharmacy, and it turned out the pills are no longer manufactured so they canceled the order; they did not even bother to call us to let us know. If I had not called, my husband would have ran out of his current medication, not knowing he was not able to fill the new RX because it is no longer manufactured, or been able to refill the old medication until another new medication was given. My husband was now, due to this still small voice, able to get his medication on a timely basis. Then I had an appointment at 10:30 a.m. I was sure it was 10:30 a.m.; I wrote it down on three different calendars. I heard His voice say, "Call and confirm."

Instead, I looked at my calendar and used that as confirmation. Ten minutes later, I heard God again; this time I called one of the people I was meeting with and she said, "No it's at 10:00 a.m." I was shocked but didn't question it. I just assumed the error was on my part. When I got to the appointment, it turns out that the time was changed that morning, exactly at the time God had told me to confirm the first time. God knew the time had changed suddenly, but He cares so much about me that He didn't want me to be late—He knows I hate being late.

- It is as if I hear God in everything I am doing. In everyday mundane tasks, I am hearing God's voice giving me ideas as to how to do the same task I have been doing for years, quicker, more efficiently, and in an all-around smarter way—with everything, even in taking out the garbage.

- Even if I fail at keeping my eyes on God often, He is still faithful to me. God's faithfulness does not depend on my actions.

- Spiritual gifts are being sharpened.

- God has brought to memory things of the past, as far back as twenty-five years ago or more that needed to be repented of. He is cleaning His temple out and taking out things that are not His, and although it may be painful to get rid of these things at the same time, it is wonderful to be replacing them with the King.

- Everyone I have prayed for has had something healed.

- It has been one full week and I have had no desire for social media; in fact, I have not even looked at it once. The need to see how and what others are doing has completely disappeared since I have found the joy of seeing and hearing what only my Father is doing through the Holy Spirit.

Day 8

I often begin prayer by saying, "I worship you, Lord." It is true, but I never took the time to understand why I did. I thought it was just a natural thing to worship God. Regardless of whether it is natural or not, it is important to take a moment and ask why. Otherwise, we may run the chance of just reciting words without that heart connection I spoke about yesterday. I understood that this happened to me. I said I worshipped God with no thought as to why, just because I knew I did. The process was uncomfortable at first because it reminded me of a past I do not care for. This is how I started my process. "Lord I worship You because You are the only God who sacrificed for me not the other way around. Lord, I worship You because You do not punish me when I stumble and turn back on my word to You. Lord, I worship You because You are the only God who has prepared good works for me since the beginning of time and intercedes for me so that I may successfully do them."

This may sound a bit like yesterday's journal, but I believe it is God teaching me how to go into my heart and really seek why I love Him. He is expanding on what I learned yesterday. In doing so, it is then that God is truly glorified through my prayers because they are no longer prayers of repetition but of passion and compassion that can only come through the Holy Spirit working in me. Give it a try some time; it will change you.

My son, do not regard lightly the discipline of the Lord, nor faint when you are reproved by Him; for those whom the Lord loves He disciplines, and He scourges every son whom He receives. (Hebrews 12:5–6)

*D*iscipline, reproof, and scourging are not words of comfort; in fact, if taken by themselves, they are painful and unpleasant. When God is in the mix, however, they take on an entirely new meaning. 1 John 4:18 says, "There is no fear in love; but perfect love casts out fear, because fear involves punishment, and the one who fears is not perfected in love." When God speaks to us and uses these words, He is not intending to punish us but to discipline us as a loving father would discipline a child.

Today I experienced reproof, discipline, and dare I even say scourging from the Lord. Throughout the day I was gently reminded of sins I had done that needed repentance. I had not repented of them earlier because, frankly, I didn't know they were sins. Sometimes, lines can get blurred. Things are so commonly accepted in today's world that when we do them we do not even give them a second thought. That is until it is brought to our attention that it is not godly behavior. That, my friends, is the kind of thing that happened today. As I drove through town doing everyday life, running errands, keeping medical appointments, grocery shopping, etc., my eyes would focus on something and that something, whatever it was, would bring back a memory. I'd smile for a moment and think, *Oh, that was a good day.* Then just as quickly the Lord would remind me of something I had said or thought during that event. Things I did not realize were sins all of sudden were very clear that they were indeed sins and they needed to be repented of immediately. The Lord reminded me of the pride I carried that day; on another time, He reminded me of a snap judgment I made. These are just two examples, but I share them with you because in both cases no one knew. I just thought of it. No harm, right? Well, that's what I thought. I was wrong. As the Lord pointed out, when I make a judgment against someone, it is really pride that is rising up. Pride is a sin; in fact, it is the same sin that got Lucifer kicked out of heaven.

The evening ended with a prayer meeting at church. I was almost out the door when someone whom I love dearly shared their wisdom with me. This person in their kindness shared their experience with me and knowledge on giving things to God. At first, I was thinking, *Oh, oh, this person is mad; I've messed up.*

As this person was sharing with me, I could almost feel God put His arm around me and say, "Listen."

At that point, I knew it was God scourging. You see, this particular person is someone whom I deeply care for. Therefore, their words carry a great weight. In the natural, I felt as if I was being reprimanded. In the natural, it hurt; I felt like saying, "Don't you know I'm trying?"

The moment, however, that I realized it was God, an amazing peace came over me, my defenses went down, and I was able to really listen to what this person was saying out of love for me. Why? Because perfect love casts out all fear. When I realized it was God, I knew instantly that I was not being scolded but rather disciplined and taught so that I could walk in a new level of holiness. Honestly, I think this is what today was all about, holiness. God cannot be where sin is. Holiness and unholiness cannot stand together—a house divided against itself will fall. God is cleaning out the parts of me that had not yet been given over to cleanliness through repentance.

As I seek to draw near to God by keeping my thoughts on Him more often and taking my thoughts captive God is drawing near to me. God has shown me what to repent of so that I can have more room for Him in my heart. It is awesome, it is like a spring cleaning for the soul. I am so happy that I serve a God that loves me so much that rather than leaving me or being disgusted by me chooses to point out the issues and helps me get rid of them. He reminds me that He took my sin at the cross already, past, present, and future. There is no need for me to carry it. He loves you that much too!

By the way, just so you know, at the end of the night, God rewarded my obedience with a present. I had taken my thoughts captive to the obedience of Christ by reciting Hebrews 12:6, "God chastens those He loves and scourges every son which He receives." I know God loves me and no lie from Satan is going to change that.

Remember, He is a rewarder of those that seek Him. Although I am seeking God for the sake of knowing and loving Him, it is okay if God gives me a reward. God is a good God and He is also my Papa. I do indeed come expectantly every day. To me, the best reward is simply His presence, but today I got a little more from Papa. The evening ended with someone giving me a large donation to fund a mission trip I am planning to take. The funds were not deserved or even imagined. As I have said before, God knows the desires of your heart. If you delight yourself in Him, He will bring them to pass. That is His promise. I have delighted more with Him this past week than I ever have my whole life. God also knows the deep desire that I have to go to the nations. He has proven faithful yet once more. His goodness is beyond imaginable.

Day 10

*A*fter my morning worship time with the Lord, I had the urge to ask God for a word for the day. I heard, "You shall be victorious."

At first, I thought, *Well, that's a good word.*

Then I realized to have a victory, there must be a battle…and a battle there was. As of now, I have not seen the victory. In fact, if I take my eyes off Jesus, all I see is pain and destruction. God in His goodness has given me this word to hold on to because He knew just what was going to happen today and what will happen in the days to come. Although what is going on right now is painful to experience, I can say with all honesty that there is a peace that I have right now that I never experienced before when I had to encounter a similar situation in the past. The difference being that this time I did not let my mind wonder imagining all the bad ways this situation could end with. Instead, every time I thought about this particular situation I took my thoughts captive. I did this by asking God the following question, "God, how do you see this situation ending?" Then God would speak to me either through a Scripture, a vision, a feeling/knowing or just a thought. Then I would thank Him and pray in agreement with what I had just heard. God knows the beginning from the end in all things. Going directly to God instead of fretting and worrying gave me a peace that I had not enjoyed the last time something similar happened.

I look forward to experiencing new ways of seeking God and drawing nearer to Him. His voice is so much clearer now. Even if I believe it may be my thoughts, I've learned these past ten days to believe that God is in me and thus His thoughts may sometimes sound like my thoughts because He loves it when I partner with Him. If I ask God for a word or for help, I am now believing in faith that the first thing I hear or think is from Him. Of course, we are to test the word. At any point in time, we as believers are hearing three voices; ours, the enemies' (Satan and his demons), and God's if you have accepted Him as savior. If what you first hear after asking God something is not a negative or an ungodly thought, then it's probably okay to accept it is God speaking to you. It becomes more of a challenge when you ask God something and the response is unconventional or what you have been praying for, then doubts sneak in. Thus, these past ten days I've been on faith, accepting that the first thought I get when I ask God something is truly God speaking, no matter how strange it may sound.

I have tried this faithfully for ten days, and every single time, it truly has been the voice of God. I know because the outcome has always worked out better than imagined. Here is an example from today: I received a text regarding some bad news I didn't know how to deal with at the moment. I asked God to tell me how to respond. I typed just what He said. It didn't make sense to me but I was obedient. A few hours later, I had the urge to reread the text. Would you believe that I had misread a part of the text, yet the response that God had given me answered it exactly the way it should? At the time, the reply God gave me to type as a response made no sense to me because I had not properly read the text the first time, but God knew what it said and answered it superbly. God is faithful.

Day 11

I am being awakened each morning with a great expectancy and curiosity, "What will I experience God do today?"

I no longer need an alarm clock to wake up. I jump out of bed with unexplainable joy and a willingness to serve my family like never before. An excitement builds within me as the time approaches to go to "my secret place" with God and close the door. The secret place is actually my office. It is where I spend uninterrupted time with Papa.

This morning I asked Papa God for a word like I did yesterday. I heard nothing at first, then I asked again. I then heard, "I'm going to get through it."

Again, like yesterday, it was a great word, but how was I going to get through "it"? I knew exactly the situation God was speaking about. I asked God how I was going to get through this particular situation and heard nothing. An hour later, my friend Barb sent me a text that said, "I e-mailed you a word I received from God; I believe it is for you."

Wow, God heard my question and answered it. Her word had the "how" of how I was going to get through my situation. I quickly remembered not to put God in a box. I expected His answer to come the way it usually comes, an impression on my heart or a still small voice. This time it came via a friend.

God is amazing. I searched and searched for a USB charger for a gadget I have and could not find it. Then it occurred to me to ask

God. As soon as I asked, God told me exactly where to look, and you guessed it, there it was. Now in hindsight, I could say with all certainty, it did not occur to me to ask; the Holy Spirit prompted me to ask. God wants to be involved in every part of your day, even in the silly little things.

Today is the closest I've felt to God since starting this experiment. There were no physical manifestations of His presence or even any healing as I did not pray for anyone today. I believe today I reached a new level of intimacy. Someone in my household did something that I considered irresponsible. I was upset, but trying to remain focused on God, I did not say a word. As I contemplated what I would say without being hurtful or disrespectful, I felt the Lord tell me why this person behaved this way. God showed me what this person was currently struggling with. Suddenly, my perspective changed. I was no longer upset but instead I began to hurt for them and intercede. God shared a secret with me. It is as if He is trusting me more.

Something else happened today that never happened before. I read Scripture today for two hours! I read the entire gospel of Mark. Some may not think this as that big of a deal, but to me it is. I have never been able to sit with the Bible for more than twenty or thirty minutes. Yes, I read the Bible every day, but the truth is that I only read ten or fifteen minutes at a time a couple of times a day. Agreed, we are to chew on the Word and mull it over. What I am stating here is not about the ability to speed read or even to boast about being able to read for two hours straight. The point is that God has given me an unquenchable thirst to want more of Him like never before. It started with a sudden urge to know which gospel contained the most miracles. Then I just had to read it.

It is only a couple of weeks into this experiment and my time with the Lord has gone from forty minutes of worship in the morning and possibly twenty minutes of Scripture throughout the day to over an hour of worship in the morning, spontaneous worship times during the day, and lengthier time spent in Scripture. You may be thinking, *Yeah, that's nice but I don't have the time.*

Let me be the first to tell you, God will extend your day. I have gotten everything I need to get done and accomplished; I've had ample time to spend with my kids and still be reading two books for the upcoming class that begins in a couple of weeks. I have more than doubled my time with the Lord, and He has rewarded me with allowing me to accomplish all I have planned and more—all the while thinking of Him throughout the day!

Day 12

*T*oday was somewhat difficult. Concentrating on anything, including God, was not as easy as it has been and the fast has been difficult today as well. I've been craving a Boston cream donut all day...LOL. I took a nap to ignore the craving and ended up rebuking demons in my dream. Nevertheless, God's faithfulness in drawing near to me as I have been drawing near to Him is something I could count on.

I was feeling miserable the majority of the day. I had an earache, headache, stomachache, and body aches. I thought for sure I was going to catch the flu that has been going around. I cannot say that I formally prayed; in fact, it was more of just a thought. I simply thought, *"Illness, you are not welcomed in my home, not on my kids, or me or my husband; I plead the blood of Jesus on us.* Just like that, I was healed! The fever left, my stomach healed, and my ear no longer was in pain; Hallelujah, praise the Lord! In hindsight this was an excellent example of taking my thoughts captive. I could have easily partnered with the illness and said, "I'm too sick to do this or that" and then gone to bed. Instead, I replaced that thought and feeling of illness with God's truth, "By His stripes I am healed" and I took authority over the sickness. Sickness is not of God and therefore I, as a child of God have all authority to command my body to be healed in Jesus' name.

Day 13

*A*lthough the last twelve days have been amazing, I came to the realization that I was becoming satisfied with a few oil drops and a bit of gold dust. I love His manifestations, and I also understand that it is a way He communicates His nearness, but I want more of Him.

A hunger I cannot explain has been stirred up in me. It is not about works, but there is effort involved. If I want to see more of God, then I must seek harder. Last night I resolved that I was going to get up earlier and extend my worship time with Him. The kids have a day off from school today so I knew they would be sleeping in. At 6:00 a.m., I came down to my office and began to pray the names of God; this turned into a three-hour expression of love. I could not believe how fast the time went. I did not want to leave my office for fear that I would not feel His presence so tangibly outside the room. Still, I am a mom and with that comes a responsibility; besides, God will never leave me nor forsake me.

After breakfast, I took the kids to a friend's house to work on a school project while I went to the local grocery store to pick up a prescription and ingredients for dinner. As I was about to check out, I felt the Lord say, "Go into this aisle."

My first thought was, *But God, I have what I came for.*

In obedience, I went into that aisle and saw an old acquaintance. I tapped him on the shoulder and said, "Hello."

We exchanged pleasantries for a moment or so and within seconds the conversation turned to God. We spent a good thirty minutes glorifying God in what He has been doing in our lives and sharing testimonies. As we spoke, we were both being refreshed and revived. It was as if there was a Holy Spirit rain rejuvenating us. We both simultaneously commented on how powerfully we were feeling His presence. I did not want to leave my office because I did not want to leave His presence, but His presence was powerfully found at the grocery store! I suppose it makes sense; after all, we are carriers of the Holy Spirit.

After our conversation, I stood at the checkout line. I approached the clerk, and the Lord told me she was not feeling well. I asked her how she was doing and she replied, "I'm good."

Knowing what the Lord had said I replied, "Really?"

She looked at me and said, "No, I'm lying. I don't feel good." She went on to share she had a terrible dream last night. In the dream she said demons were pulling her into a dark place; she would escape and then another one would grab her.

I grabbed her hand, asked her if I could pray, and said, "In the name of Jesus, I rebuke this spirit. I break the assignment of the enemy. I bind this ungodly spirit and I release the peace of Jesus in every area of your body." Then I prayed for healing as the Lord led. The prayer was less than a minute. I asked her if she felt any different.

She said, "As you were praying, I could feel tingling, then I felt a pressure from the top of my head start to go down and then zzuuppp…it went out. I feel great now!"

Just in case you were wondering, she is a believer. What a morning this has been—a forty-second prayer and deliverance and healing occurred at register eleven of the local ShopRite, all through the name of Jesus and for His glory!

Throughout the day, I felt the need to stop what I was doing and just pray, and that's exactly what I did. This wanting to spontaneously stop what I was doing to pray, I believe is a manifestation of God drawing near to me and drawing me unto Him. Throughout the day I drew near to God every time I did something that glorified God. An example would be what happened at ShopRite. We are called to heal the sick, cast out demons, and raise the dead. I did two out of three, I drew near to God at that moment. I was drawing near to God as I shared with my friend what God was doing in my life giving God all the Glory. God is faithful, you draw near to God and God will draw near to you.

Day 14

_P_rior to salvation, I had what some would call a "potty mouth," in two languages. After salvation, I said almost no cuss words. I went from saying a cuss word several times in a conversation to perhaps a couple in a month. I thought that was pretty good. I've gotten better, but every once in a while, one slips out. I never thought much of it; if by chance a cuss word came out, then I would repent. After all, it was not as if I had set out with the intention to use a bad word and I did not use them often at all.

This morning my daughter wore what I would consider an inappropriate outfit. You may wonder why I bought it for her in the first place. Well, as a parent, we buy the best we can with what we have. However, eventually, the child grows and matures but the clothes stay the same size. It gives me a new appreciation for the Israelites that traveled with Moses…LOL. Anyway, after I saw what my daughter was wearing, I gave her one of those "here we go again" looks. She asked what was wrong and I shared my thoughts with her. She then shared her thoughts with me. Then out of my mouth came, "I don't give a @$%# what you…"

I could not finish the sentence; instantly I was grieved. It was no longer okay to say a cuss word. I was grieved to the point where I became nauseated by my words. I quickly repented, but not like before. I thought that in the past when I repented, it was sincere—I really was sorry. Today was different. It felt as if I was sorry from the deepest crevasse of my soul. God was kind; my daughter changed without even a word—I didn't even have to ask her. I believe I was grieved with such intensity because as I pursue God more and more, He is making me holy as He is holy. This is not to sound conceited, but I do believe that God is doing an internal work in me. This has not been a one-sided experiment.

On another note, I can still notice how easy it is to take my eyes off God, but how refreshing and inspiring it is to know that just as quickly as I take my eyes off Him, He is there to gently remind me to put my eyes back on the kingdom. It is becoming easier to stay focused on Him. It has been two weeks since I started this experiment, and I am happy to say that the amount of time I spend focusing on God with everything I have and do has multiplied exceedingly. I look forward to the next few weeks as I go deeper into a more intimate relationship with my friend, bridegroom, and savior Jesus, not to mention the Holy Spirit and God.

The following are some other blessings that occurred during the course of the week that I did not journal.

- You can't outgive God. The Lord said to give a certain amount to someone. I said yes. I got home late that night, but the intention was to electronically put the money in the account when I got home. This is how faithful God is. I had every intention of doing it when I got home. However, before I got home, someone handed me a letter. She told me to read it at home. When I opened it, it was exactly ten times the amount I was going to give. Listen, when God tells you to give something away, do it; it's the upside-down kingdom and you cannot outgive God.

- If you ask God for a word, He will give it, every time.

- As I seek God more, He shares more with me. For example, before a friend calls, I hear her ringtone before she actually calls. A few minutes before my husband gets home, I hear his car alarm activate, and a couple of minutes later he is actually home and activates his alarm. Perhaps, you may say I have a prophetic gift; that may be so, but it has been upgraded.

Day 15

*I*t amazes me how quickly three hours of worship, prayer, and Scripture reading passes by now. I wake up with such a hunger for the Word that I cannot describe it. Just two weeks ago I was only reading an estimated twenty minutes of Scripture a day, perhaps thirty and not in one sitting, At the most, forty minutes was spent in uninterrupted prayer and worship time, although I did pray in the Spirit throughout the day. Now, I can easily be reading Scripture for over an hour and completely lose track of time. As for worship and prayer, well I just can't get enough. I love my time with Papa. I wake up at 5:00 a.m. or earlier to get in the uninterrupted prayer time and usually go to bed sometime after 11:00 p.m., yet the day flies by as I spend it communing with my Bridegroom. I am yearning for a face-to-face encounter with the lover of my soul. I've learned I've been putting Him in a box so to speak, and He is showing me that His goodness and His ways are far beyond anything I can imagine.

Day 16

*A*t the beginning of the book, I mentioned I was doing a fast; what I did not mention was what the fast was for. One thing that I do as part of the outreach ministry I have the privilege of leading is going into hospital emergency room waiting rooms and praying for people. It can be a very difficult thing to do because of the opposition we face both spiritually and naturally. We want to do this ministry in an honorable way, and we want to be a blessing and not a burden. Therefore, when we enter a hospital, we ask permission from whomever is at the front desk. Mostly, they are agreeable. However, they too need to follow protocol; hence, they need to make security aware that we are there. This is where the opposition and spiritual warfare usually comes in. The security guards are very kind and cordial for the most part and wait until we are finished praying before they ask us to leave. To them, it is a solicitation. So, we leave. Like I said, we want to be a blessing. Besides, we are to be submissive to those in authority; after all, we are representing God.

Back to the fast. One of the things I was fasting for was for breakthrough and favor for ministering in hospitals. Today, that happened. What happened today is one of those things that you usually hear about at a Christian conference or in a movie. Today, I experienced God's favor like I never thought imaginable. Within this time of fasting, I heard the Lord say, "Volunteer through the pastoral department."

I thought, "*Well God, I am licensed, but I don't know if that necessarily makes me a pastor.*"

I must admit I was not obedient right away; I actually waited a few days and then decided to print out volunteer forms for a local hospital. This morning we were going to visit a woman we have been sharing God's love with at a nursing home/rehab. I had volunteered there several years ago, and I was given a very limited number of people I was allowed to see. This was about six years ago. Fast-forward to this morning. As I was preparing to go to see this woman, the Lord impressed upon my heart to volunteer at this nursing home/rehab hospital. I had not thought about doing that again, but I had nothing to lose. God said it and my job is to say, "Yes Papa, I will do whatever you want me to do."

I called and was asked to come in for an interview. I have heard of God's favor before, but I have never experienced it to this degree. What happened today is unheard of and can only be possible through God Almighty. I don't want to bore you with many details, so I will cut right down to the chase. I was given free rein to pray for everyone in the hospital, no limits. I am allowed to freely share the gospel and give communion, and we will be given one hour a month every month for a healing/prayer service and we will be allowed to hold a separate prayer/healing service for the staff. That is unprecedented favor!

I once heard a pastor say that we are being chased down by God's favor and that incredible things are waiting for us if we believe and if we seek. I, like most of you, believed that it was for other people. After today, however, I know it's for other people, for me, and for you!

I haven't done anything but keep my eyes on His kingdom the best I can, which includes many slipups, but God doesn't care about the mistakes, He cares that you are trying with all your heart, mind, and strength. Today, I received an answer to personal prayer as well as an answer to corporate prayer. Our church has been interceding for a way to evangelize outside the church and bring Christ's love to many.

It was as if the seas parted right in front of me, all the opposition, spiritual or otherwise, was pushed to the side and God was marching in front of me saying, "This is my beloved daughter, give her all she wants; I've paid for it already."

I am telling you, this kind of stuff does not just happen!

As if that was not enough, we led someone to Christ today, and he wants to be water-baptized, hallelujah! God's presence fell on us so powerfully as we walked and left the nursing home worshipping that we could barely stand straight by the time we got to the car. We spent at least twenty minutes worshipping, praising, and thanking God for what He had done. It was all Him, all from His favor, and all glory goes to God.

God has increased my faith, God hears us and answers us, He overwhelms me with His favor, and all I've done is simply love Him; wow, it's amazing.

God is multi-faceted. I personally believe that you can focus on just one aspect of God and spend a lifetime experiencing Him in different ways just through that one facet you are focusing on. For example, you may be focusing on God as Jehovah-Jireh, the provider, and God can manifest His provision in so many ways that we could live a lifetime exploring it and still could not exhaust all the different ways He provides. He is an infinite God with infinite ways. Following that line of thought, I realized that I do not just want to focus on one aspect, but I want to experience as much of God as possible—I want to try new things that are revealed in Scripture as ways of relating to God.

There are many Scripture verses referring to rest. Exodus 33:14 states that He will give us rest when we are in His presence. Psalm 37:7 tells us to be still and wait patiently on the Lord. If I dwell in His shelter, I will rest in His shadow according to Psalm 91:1. In Isaiah 40:28–31 we learn that if we rest on the Lord, we will not grow weary, we will soar like eagles, and we will run and not be tired. Another Scripture states to be still and know that He is God. There are more Scriptures, but the point is that God tells us to rest in Him. In it there is power. As we rest in the Lord, we silence ourselves and that involves putting our flesh to death and allowing our own spirit to commune with God. It is a difficult thing to just sit there and not do anything, not even pray, and to just rest and enjoy His presence.

I recently heard a teaching on rest and through it, I learned that although it may feel like nothing is happening, there really is something happening in the spiritual. The proof that something happened is how you finish after your "resting" time. The result should be inner peace, a changed mindset, and a closeness to God among other things.

Resting in God is another way of achieving intimacy with God. When we rest in God we take the thoughts that stress us out (taking our thoughts captive) and we give them to God knowing that they are burdens that Jesus already paid for at the cross. As we rest in God and give Him all our woes we empty ourselves out and make room for the Holy Spirit to come and fill us afresh, that is God drawing near to us. In this place of rest, as we draw near to God and God draws near to us, it becomes easier to feel His presence. Sometimes I can even feel His hugs, I can hold His hand and feel Him holding mine back. It is an intimacy and a security that is yours anytime when you submit your thoughts to Him.

I found this to be a difficult task. I put on old Christian hymns, I closed my eyes, and I tried to focus on the lyrics that told of Jesus, God's goodness, and His sacrifice. The key word here was tried. Immediately my flesh was annoyed. I wanted to check my e-mail and clean off my desk, and I started thinking about homework, and other things. Eventually, I was able to focus. I was awake, yet I felt as if I was asleep. I was peaceful, and I started to get visions and prophetic words. Then I had an image in my mind of my feet being in water. It was then my eyes popped open; a few seconds later my daughter started calling, "Mommy, come upstairs I need you."

The toilet had overflowed. Immediately, I was standing in an inch of water. Not exactly what I thought the vision was supposed to mean. Here is where God comes in. Usually, this kind of thing would have driven me crazy. I probably would have yelled at my daughter for not cleaning it up and just freaked out altogether, but that did not happen. I started to mop and a moment or two into it, I remembered the vision. I was full of joy. I was calm. I was laughing and singing while I was mopping. I usually dislike mopping quite a bit.

I believe God gave me a prophetic picture of what was about to happen. He also filled me with the tranquility and joy that I needed to deal with the situation. God is awesome. He wants to partner with us and tell us things to come. John 15:15 states that God calls us friends and tells us things: "No longer do I call you slaves, for the slave does not know what his master is doing; but I have called you friends, for all things that I have heard from My Father I have made known to you."

Day 18

The more time I spend fellowshipping with God, the more I learn about Him. Throughout this book, I have referred to James 4:8 a few times. If I draw near to God, He will draw near to me. Yes, it is most definitely true that He will, but there is no striving involved on my part. In fact, I draw near to Him because He first drew me. John 6:44 states, "No one can come to Me unless the Father who sent Me draws him; and I will raise him up on the last day."

God started. He called me first. God quickened my spirit. I became alive at the sound of His voice as my spirit jumped into excitement urging me to go closer to God. It sounds like a love story, does it not? Now the book of Song of Solomon makes sense. Jesus, our bridegroom, waits for us to be ready; in the meantime, He prepares a place for us in His kingdom, and in Him, we then become one as the Holy Spirit indwells us. There is a lot more to being the bride of Christ. If you want to learn more on the subject, I recommend reading, *The Bride of Christ, The Bridegroom, and His Bride*, by Christopher W. Hussey.

I have become more aware of my thoughts and language throughout these past 18 days. When someone we respect is in the room, we speak differently not because we cannot be ourselves but because we want to honor that person. It is the same with God. Now that I am being made more aware of His presence around me, I know that everything I say He hears and everything I think He knows. He is right beside me. God always was, but now I actually realize it as a truth in my life that should not be ignored. In turn, I am the one getting the blessing. I am becoming a better person. I am more aware of how I treat people and even of my tone of voice and sarcasm.

I am more aware of Him. As I am watching TV or conversing with my kids, I can feel His presence come near. It is hard to explain. The best I can describe is that it feels like a combination of warmth, goose bumps, and a weight. Sometimes it is those things individually and sometimes it is a combination of them, but it is wonderful and comforting. Sometimes I am so overwhelmed I just begin to tear up. God Himself is approaching me, and at that moment, I had not done anything to deserve it or to earn it—He came just because He loves me.

*A*s I entered the pastor's office for morning intercession before service, I felt the Lord say, "Something great is going to happen." I thought that was a word for the church; little did I know it was a word for me personally. I started off the morning by waking up late; apparently, I set the alarm on my phone but did not hit the save button. Then after ironing my husband's clothes, he told me I ironed the wrong pants—the pants I had ironed were what he called his summer pants, and they were too thin to wear in January. Frankly, I thought they looked like all his other pants. Unfortunately, he told me this as I am kissing him goodbye with keys in hand ready to leave for church. Since I have been pressing into God, taking as many thoughts captive to God, things have been very different. Before now, I would have flipped out over waking up late—I am a very punctual person and I give myself no tolerance for tardiness. Before today, if my husband would have told me I ironed the wrong pants, I would have given him the iron and walked away. None of my usual responses came into play. I was actually shocked at my own response. I was not stressed when I woke up late which is a huge thing for me. Also, when my husband mentioned the wrong pants were ironed, I did something I never thought I would have done, at least not with a happy heart. I took off my jacket, grabbed another pair of pants, and ironed those with such joy that it took me by surprise.

While at church service during the worship time, I was singing along with everyone else then it occurred to me, I was not only singing to a God that was sitting on some throne high in the heavens, rather I was also singing to a God who was standing right in front of me through the Holy Spirit. Let me tell you, if that does not change your perspective on worship, nothing will! When I realized I was singing to God and He was in fact right there listening; my heart almost exploded with admiration. I could no longer stand and sing; I had to kneel in reverence.

I am about to share with you a short story from my childhood in order that you may understand the magnitude of the breakthrough God gave me today in something that I have struggled with since I was a child.

When I was about five or six years old, my grandfather had a massive stroke. The stroke left my grandfather paralyzed on one side of his body; he was no longer able to speak and was left with the mentality of a toddler. I was only told that grandpa was placed in a special hospital and I was not allowed to see him. This devastated me as my grandfather and I were close. The special hospital was a nursing home/hospital for the severely disabled. My mother did not handle my grandfather's stroke very well. She would not allow me to visit my grandfather because she said that I was too young and could not handle what I would see. She went on to tell me that he was nothing like I remembered him and he now made noises instead of speaking and would get very emotional. I would not be able to handle it because it was very scary, she would tell me. Then she would add more fear by telling me that everyone else in that hospital was also scary and that I would have nightmares if I went in. That was that—mom had spoken and I had to obey. My mom, dad, and brothers were allowed to see him, while I waited in the waiting area crying because I could not see my grandfather, yet at the same time with some relief because mom said that what I would see would be so scary I would have nightmares the rest of my life; not the thing to say to a six-year-old little girl who was already confused as to what happened to her beloved grandfather. No one had ever explained what a stroke actually was to me at that time. In my eyes, grandpa was perfectly fine one day and the next he was a disabled toddler in the body of an eighty-year-old man who now wanted nothing to do with me. Yes, my mother told me that if I were to visit him, he would become very emotional and that would be worse for his health and something worse could happen to him.

One day I was in the waiting room of this nursing home/hospital and an older gentleman about the age of my grandfather sitting in a wheelchair with no legs saw me at a distance and started to smile at me. I smiled back, then he smiled more. Within seconds he was doing a comedy routine for me from afar. I was laughing, and for the first time, somehow I felt close to my grandfather again. Then my mother came down from his room, saw me smiling and laughing with this stranger, and yelled at me. She told me that it was dangerous to hang out with "someone like that." She told me I didn't know what he had and I should make no contact with anyone in that hospital. She yanked me by the arm and we left. This story is not to put my mother in a bad light. She loved the best she could and unfortunately has lived a life full of fear. She passed that fear on to me that day. After that day, I was afraid of being around someone disabled. I would avoid severely disabled people at all cost because I could accidentally make things worse for them.

Now fast-forward to today. Today I was asked to pray for a relative of a friend. The person we were praying for we were told broke her hip and was now in surgery and disabled. As an adult, I have volunteered at nursing homes and was around disabled people often, but I was unprepared for what I encountered when I got to the hospital. When I walked in, the first thing I saw were the parents. Both had puffy red eyes from crying, both were exhausted, and both were trying their best to keep it together. Then I looked at the bed and saw the woman I had gone in to pray for, and I just froze. It took a few seconds to even get my voice back. All of a sudden, I was a little girl again afraid to touch the disabled person for fear that I may make it worse. As I took a step back and asked God for strength, I heard the Lord say, "Look at her."

I looked at this woman who was in a neck brace and with all sorts of gizmos and gadgets attached to her body in order to monitor her and her legs tightly wrapped to keep her from moving that hip; she did not have the capacity to speak or communicate; yet when I locked eyes with her, all I could see was the most beautiful girl. My heart was pouring out love for her; all the fear disappeared. God gave me a compassion I never had and took away a fear I always had that had been sitting dormant all those years and allowed me to speak with a tenderness I did not even know I was capable of having. All fear was gone and I was able to minister to her and the mother.

God did a work in me today, a work that was needed and I didn't even know it. When the visit was over, as my prayer partner and I were waiting for the elevator, I confessed to what I had felt and I thanked her for coming with me. As I confessed my fear, the Lord brought back this memory of me in the nursing home as a child as the rest of my family visited my grandfather. I had not thought about that day since I was a little girl. Through God's grace, I was able to forgive my mother for separating me from my grandfather and for transferring her fear on to me. That, in turn, allowed me to deal with the fear I was also carrying. I confessed fear as sin, renounced it, broke the agreement with it, and took back any authority I had given to fear in my life, and I asked God to fill me with His faith and truth. God healed me today. As I look back on this week, I realize that God has also redeemed something that had been lost in my life. My grandfather died in that nursing home. I was not even allowed to go to the funeral; I was too young was what I was told. Almost three years passed between the time my grandfather had the stroke and when he died and I never got to see him. However, a few days ago, God gave me full access to pray for anyone and everyone at a nursing home/rehab hospital. Perhaps, in God's tender mercies He healed me today of the emotional wound I had been carrying so that I could properly do the ministry He has given me.

I firmly believe that it is because I have been seeking His face and He has been drawing me in that I was able to see His hand throughout this whole day. Despite my shortcomings, He still used me, and the mother of this woman whom I prayed for was healed of knee pain and God touched her heart as we ministered regarding a broken heart. God's presence was in the room. As we prayed instantly, the disabled young lady calmed down, burdens were lifted from the parents, and healing came.

I am now more aware of God's presence; God is allowing me to see His hand at work in everything I do. He is opening my eyes. Seeing God move in areas I may not have noticed before is bringing me to higher levels of faith. His presence brings peace to every situation. It is wonderful to end your day knowing that God was with you every step of the way and believing it with every ounce of your mortal being.

Day 20

I've heard many say that when the victory comes, I need to prepare myself for the attack of the enemy. Today in my time with the Lord, He's confirmed that those words are a fear tactic from the enemy himself. Yes, I may face opposition and some of it may be harsh and dreadful opposition but regardless, God is my Savior, He has my back, and He has equipped me. It is not "the higher the level, the bigger the devil", as they say, rather it is the higher the level, the bigger the anointing God will give me to complete the work He has given me.

This morning I woke up extra early with a desire to read Scripture. I read until it was time for the children to get up for school. The next hour or so was spent getting things ready for the day and getting the kids off to school. After they left, I went into the office to continue my time with the Lord. Over three hours passed and it felt as if it was only 20 minutes. Every day, as God draws me closer to Him, His presence becomes more real to me. It was as if He was a real person standing in the room with me telling His secrets, things to come, things I should do, and things about other people so that I could intercede for them.

Perhaps, you may be thinking, *This woman is crazy; she's just imagining this.*

But am I? This morning the Lord gave me a vision of a large field. "The fields are white for picking, start praying for the harvesters."

That's what I felt the Lord say to me today. What you don't know is that for the past two years, at least I have been praying for ways to pray in hospitals and for the government and places like police stations and fire stations. I want to pray and bless those who locally sacrifice their lives for us every day. The police stations have been just as difficult to pray at as the hospitals. Today after that vision and word, the Lord said to go to the local state trooper office and tell them what is on my heart. God has not led me wrong yet, so I did just that. I could not believe it. The state troopers based in my town are allowing me as a representative of my church and minister of the Gospel to serve them breakfast and pray for their needs and their protection. This is a breakthrough that only God could have done. The past two years I have been beating my head against a wall, as they say, with nothing to show for it. As I am becoming more aware of the Holy Spirit, I am beginning to understand how He talks to me and how to be obedient to His Word. The confidence I have in knowing that God is with me and is telling me what to do or not to do has given me the strength to go outside my comfort zone and do things I never thought I would do. I have, if you will, a holy boldness that has come only from God. This was another thing I was fasting for, a breakthrough in government agencies, particularly with policemen.

I am not implying that every single move I do I stop and ask God; that would be silly. We are to mature in our faith. As we grow in Christ, there must be a level of trust that evolves where we know that we have a firm foundation, and so instead of asking constantly if you should do this or do that, we just move forward but with a listening ear so that we are constantly aware of His promptings. There are, of course, times where we will seek Him more than others, but remember, we are after His presence and intimately knowing Him. If we persist in our relationship with Christ by knowing Him through His Word—both logos and rhema—then we begin to know how He thinks, thus making the process of taking our thoughts captive an automatic process, leading to a transformation that forms us more into the image of Christ.

God's faithfulness is so overwhelming. At the same time, realizing how much I need to be dependent on God is sobering. Still, it is complete joy finding myself wanting to be completely submissive to His will. This has come with challenges, but God is merciful, loving, and a good Father. It seems that God does not only reward success but He rewards the attempt. The attempt can be translated into faith. I attempt things now because I have faith that God is indeed speaking to me and as His sheep; I can hear His voice. I have faith that He loves me more than any one person ever can; therefore, He will not lead me astray. I have faith that even if I mishear or I make a mess of things, God will still use it for His glory. The Holy Spirit is the kindest person you will ever meet. When I make a mess of things, He is gentle in correcting; oh, it is so encouraging!

Day 21

Knowing that the Holy Spirit is with you every single second of the day is the most amazing feeling. It is an amazing feeling because you never have a reason to be scared, you never have a reason to doubt that whatever spiritual gift you may need in ministry will be given at the exact time, and best of all, you never ever feel abandoned or alone. Whether I spend three hours in worship or five minutes, it does not matter; God will never leave me nor forsake me. If you spend five minutes with God because you love Him and you just want to spend time with Him, it is worth so much more than if you spend four hours reading the Bible just because you think you have to. It is all about love. His love for me causes me to love Him back. This is how my relationship is growing more intimately with God. I am falling deeper in love with Him. When you are in love with someone you trust them, you believe them, they can do no wrong. It is just like that with Jesus, but better. Jesus is not a human therefore He will never let you down. You will never feel unloved again once you get to know your Savior, Jesus.

Today God highlighted someone in a crowded room and gave me a word of knowledge about them. The person was shocked at how accurate the word was, but she was more shocked when I told her that God only revealed it not to bring her sin to the light but rather to heal her hurting heart. Once she realized how much our Father in heaven loved her, this woman was able to let go of nineteen years of bitterness, hatred, and anger by forgiving a person that had left her mother widowed and destroyed her childhood and essentially her life up to this point. It is important to know that forgiveness does not mean that what the person did to you is right nor does it mean that if you forgive, you won't feel the hurt. Forgiveness is giving it to God and getting out of the way so that God can be the judge and not you. We are not to judge anyone—that will make us the Lord and we are not Lord of anything, only God is. Unforgiveness is a sin of idolatry and pride when we judge someone because we make ourselves judge and we think we know better than God.

Again tonight, I could feel the Holy Spirit drawing near to me as I sat on the couch with my husband. There was a peace over me that felt like one of those lead vests they put over you at the dental office when taking X-rays. It was a warm weight that would come and go in waves. It was a warming of my body from the inside-out. It was as if I could hear God say, "I know the plans I have for you; you will like them; they are plans for you to prosper. Do not worry, I have your back."

Amidst financial issues, health issues, and plumbing issues, the Holy Spirit stepped in and soothed my soul. Proverbs 3:5 has come alive for me tonight: "Trust in the Lord with all your heart and lean not on your own understanding." God gives us these verses but also empowers us by His grace to believe them. With my own eyes, I may not be able to see a positive outcome to these situations, but God's peace allows me to trust God. I don't have to rely on my understanding of the problem; I have to rely on God. This becomes easier to do as we get to know God more and spend time with Him. The Scriptures state that God calls me friend. I actually believe that now.

The following are some other blessings that occurred during the course of the week that I have not journaled:

- I find with every passing day that I want to know the holy Trinity more. It's not just God the Father or just Jesus or just the Holy Spirit. I know it is all one and the same God but they are different aspects of Him. I want to know these aspects in depth. I find myself crying out to God for a fresh baptism of fire, more empowerment through His Holy Spirit, a fresh infilling of the Spirit. It's all I can think about. I've heard His voice so clearly these past weeks and I know there is more to come. I anxiously wait, knowing that God will manifest Himself, but how? Will it be through a word of knowledge, through a physical manifestation of His presence like oil, or perhaps through a prophetic word that comes to pass? Truthfully, I do not know and do not care. I will rejoice as much in a word of knowledge that heals a boo-boo on a thumb as I will in a miracle that causes a blind eye to see. It's not about what He does; it is about why He does it. God does it because He loves us.

    When my husband and I were dating, the tiniest gesture was taken as an act of love, and I accepted each gift knowing it came from a place of wanting to get to know me better, wanting to spend the rest of his life with me. It is the same with God for me. What may seem like a tiny gesture to some, a word of knowledge or a headache being healed, is still a manifestation of the Creator of the world invading my world. I've repented for taking for granted the gifts of the Spirit; they are not only gifts but God Himself working through me. I had lost reverence for the Lord and did not even know it. One should be careful not to take the things of the Lord for granted; He is a Holy God and worthy to be praised, for everything.

- My faith has been built up. When I pray now, I picture Jesus right in front of me. There is no doubt at all in me that He is hearing my prayer. There is a surety and a calmness that comes in knowing that He has heard my prayer and I can trust that God has my back. All I have to say is, "Yes Papa, I will do what you want me to do." The exciting thing is that not only can I hear what God wants me to do but also there is no fear of doing it.

It's God that is in charge, not me; there is no pressure. I can pray for healing or anything really and know that God will move. Perhaps, His answer may be not now or I have something better for you, which translates into a no, but that's okay. I am learning to completely trust God.

The more I hear the voice of God, the easier it is to recognize the voice of the enemy and not partner with it.

Day 22

This morning I woke up to the words, "I love you extravagantly." I thought it was my husband and thought, *That's new and weird.*

My husband loves me, but he is a silent conservative type of guy. Gushy words are not something he is known for. Nevertheless, I rolled over in bed to kiss him and say thank you and he was not even in the room. Then I realized it was the Lord that had said it. I do not know what God means when He says, "extravagantly"; the truth is I do not know what loving extravagantly would look like, but I took Him at His word. It was a word spoken by God right into my heart that prepared me for the day to come. God is speaking to me as His bride. He is waking me up in the morning with a tender loving word. I no longer need to be the one to initiate the conversation hoping that maybe I would hear something from God. God will say kind things just because He loves me and I am the apple of His eye. I believe God has always been saying these things to me as His love for me has never changed. He will never love me less and He cannot love me more than what He already does. However, I do believe that now I can hear them and accept them because the lies I had been believing about myself and even God have been broken by taking my thoughts captive and replacing those lies with biblical truths. James 4:7, "Submit yourselves, then, to God. Resist the devil, and he will flee from you" is a biblical truth I have been washing my mind with. For example, when a thought comes into my mind that I will have another mini-stroke, I submit to God by repenting of fear and I resist the devil by confessing the truth, by His stripes I am healed. Eventually the enemy will get tired and he will leave me alone. The same love God has for me is the same love He has for you. All this is available to you too.

Tomorrow my schedule is full of places to go and people to pray for; it is something I love to do, yet at the same time I am doing it now with the authority of a licensed minister and leading and taking a team of prayer warriors with me. As I thought about it, I admit I quickly realized just how unqualified I feel. At the risk of completely agreeing with fear, I decided to sit and wait on the Lord. Ten minutes passed and it felt like thirty, and twenty minutes passed and it felt like an hour. My time in the secret place with God was challenging to say the least, and God was not the problem. God was faithfully waiting for me to get rid of whatever was not of Him so that He could move in and do what He loves to do, love His child. After roughly forty minutes waiting on the Lord, I was getting very fidgety, and as I was about to get up and start praying because I thought I had to be the one to do something (of course I was wrong), I heard the Lord say, "Sit and wait some more."

Not long after, I got a vision of big bold print words "JOSHUA 8:1." The words took up the whole room. I immediately looked it up. "Then the Lord said to Joshua, "Do not be afraid; do not be discouraged. Take the whole army with you, and go up and attack Ai. For I have delivered into your hands the king of Ai, his people, his city, and his land." This word was the encouragement that built up my faith. I was at that point feeling discouraged and afraid. The name of the evangelistic team that I have the privilege of leading is called "God's army" and tomorrow we will be praying for a group of people who have authority over our city. I believe through this verse, God was speaking to me saying, "Do not be afraid or discouraged; take your team to the places I have sent you and I will give you that place and favor with its people."

This is the first time for me personally where I asked God for an answer and He directed me to a Scripture verse that declared a promise over the situation. That is extravagant love. I would have been just as content if I would have just heard Him say it will go well. God in His infinite mercy and love instead gave me a promise in a verse that is specific to the outreach team and what we're doing and even addressed how I was feeling at the time. Some of you may be skeptical and are thinking, *Well, she probably had that verse memorized and that's why she thought of it;* well, let me assure you that I don't even recall ever reading that verse. This was all God. To Him be all praise and glory.

Another new thing I experienced today was His voice amidst chaos. In the eyes of any unbeliever and maybe even in the eyes of some believers it looked as if nothing was going right. The whole day was one interruption after another. Yet, through it all, God guided my words and even my thoughts in such a way that all has worked out. Not a harsh word came out of my mouth, no anger was expressed, and best of all, those I interacted with felt loved. He is Jehovah-Jireh my provider and He has and will provided all I need to get through the day.

Day 23

*Y*esterday's prophetic word of Joshua 8:1 was partially fulfilled. The people we prayed with today that have a large measure of authority in the town I live in and in neighboring towns have given us the green light to pray for them. It is yet another open door. God has given me favor in the spiritual realm and with man. Was it anything done from my own power? No. I do, however, accredit it to seeking God and hearing His voice and obeying it. Frankly, I am only now realizing how much I depended on my own strength and intelligence, which usually led to me doing things the hard way. Through this "forty-day experiment," I am learning to fine-tune God's voice. I know it now right away. When I do something that I know I heard God say, I do it confidently knowing that no matter what the results look like, it will have a good outcome that glorifies God. What happens between the first step and the outcome does not stress me out. My confidence is now on God and not in my own abilities. Things are now happening that I did not see happening this quickly and this well. It is all because when God draws near, I now know it. I am no longer oblivious to it and I am able to communicate with Him in full faith knowing He is listening and will answer. Overall, life is happier and more peaceful.

Day 24

*T*oday was a Proverbs 16:9 kind of a day. "The mind of man plans his ways, but the Lord directs his steps." I like schedules. The easiest way to ruffle my feathers is to disrupt my schedule. Earlier this week the Lord had put on my heart to invite a few people who He had highlighted over for a time of worship and praise. I did what I was asked and invited these people over. This morning I realized that what the Lord had asked me to do would change my schedule. Suddenly, I was very selfish of my time. I did not want to share my alone time with God. The mornings were my time to worship. Not a very godly attitude, I know; I repented. As I was torn between what the Lord had asked me to do and what I wanted to do, the Lord gently reminded me that it didn't matter who was in the room; they could not take away from my time with Him unless I allowed it. That was a good point but not one that I was ready to believe.

God knows the needs of everyone and He also knows their desires. As we draw near to God, He shares the needs and desires of others with us so that we may partner with God in blessing that person. Each one of the people that came, who God had highlighted, was hungering for time with Him but found it difficult to do it on their own. We worshipped over an hour with no talking and no snacking, just pure admiration for God. As for me, I was selfish of my time with God because it had been difficult for me to express emotion for God in public. Only recently did I allow my daughter to worship with me; that in itself was big for me. God was right, inviting the people did not take away my time with Papa. I danced, I sang, I declared, and I rejoiced more than ever. It was a beautiful time with the Lord and my friends that I would have missed out on if I had not listened to Papa's gentle correction.

It is true what they say—God is always talking. I have written a few times about the peace I have been experiencing, but today I had joy, a lot of it. Twice today that I know of Satan or his minions tried to take that joy away. The first instance was through someone's careless words. I started to feel hurt by this person's words and felt as if I had done something wrong even though I did not and don't think that was the intention of this person. However, just as I was starting to feel bad, the Lord started to have a conversation with me. Usually, it has been that I start the conversation with God through prayer or by straight out asking God a question. This time it was different. As I started to spiral down the road of rejection, the Lord intercepted my thoughts with His truth. The Lord reminded me of the other conversations I have had with this person throughout the week. Then the Holy Spirit pointed out key words that this person was using that showed that I was loved and honored in a godly way. Then the Holy Spirit showed me different reasons why this person spoke the way they did. He turned my sadness into joy again. The second instance happened as I was going home. As I was about to turn on to my street, the Lord told me to slow down. I slowed down to almost a stop and was just rolling down the road when I heard my daughter scream, "Mommy, stop!"

Due to blinding sunlight, I almost hit a car. If I had been going just a mile or two faster, I would not have been able to stop because as I was taking the turn, she had ran the stop sign. I was so thankful my daughter was with me to scream stop and that God had told me to slow down just moments before.

Drawing near to God as the Holy Spirit draws me in has proven to me that God is always speaking and this forty-day experiment has allowed me to hear God's voice clearly even when I am not even trying to listen. The kindness of God is available 24/7.

God's kindness is never-ending. The Holy Spirit's gentleness is beyond description. Today, as I took my teenage daughter clothes shopping, something that usually stresses me out, I could hear the Holy Spirit tell me, "You did well, I'm proud of you," as I waited for her in the dressing room.

As I heard His voice multiple times telling me kind things, I could feel His presence and His overwhelming peace and joy. This is the very first time I have ever taken one of my kids clothes shopping that I did not come back completely frazzled. It is not that my children misbehave; rather it is because I usually feel like an incompetent mom. Often, I get easily overwhelmed when there are too many people or mirrors in a store and I get migraines and become very dizzy. By the time the kids are done shopping, I am ready to pass out and in all truth, sometimes, I get irritated with myself because I cannot afford to give them what I would like them to have. None of that happened today. Throughout the day, God was speaking to me, keeping me focused on Him. Somewhere within the past twenty-five days, there was a transition that took place; I am no longer struggling to hear God nor am I being the one to initiate the conversation. It is like having your best friend with you all the time but only better. The Holy Spirit is the kindest person I know and I love Him so much.

Day 26

The Holy Spirit knows me better than anybody else. Knowing He is there makes the difference between feeling rejected by everyone around you and feeling so loved by God that you do not care who is around you and what they are thinking. The Holy Spirit always knows exactly what I need and what you need too. I may think I know what I want or need, but when I do not get it, I have a choice to be either offended at God or say, "Papa, you said you have a plan for me, it is a good plan for my welfare and not my calamity and so I give this thought of what I want up to you," and say, "I know you have something better for me Papa." Then take comfort in the fact that my heavenly Father does indeed have better for me.

This confidence in God is part of the intimacy that is growing in my relations with God. Intimacy requires trust. I am learning to trust God more, which means my faith is growing. It is my responsibility to edify myself through the Spirit and find comfort in God. My situation cannot change the reality of God's word.

Tonight, the Holy Spirit comforted me in the best way, hugs. I was at a conference feeling a bit alone since my husband had decided to stay home. People were going out of their way to get to me and give me a hug. A couple of people actually said, "I don't know why Holy Spirit just said to give you a hug." God knows exactly what you need. He is indeed a loving Father.

*I*t has been a little over three weeks since I started this experiment on intimacy with God. It has been great but not without its battles. To take one's thoughts captive to the obedience of Christ, it is important to know God's word and your identity in Him. If you do not know what God says and thinks about you, how can you battle against thoughts of unworthiness, condemnation, and defeat or any negative thought for that matter?

This morning as I was looking forward to my time in worship, I heard the enemy's voice in my head, "You are going to get bored. Are you really worshipping or just going through a routine?"

The thought was discouraging for a moment. The Lord then whispered, "But I like it when you spend time with me."

Biblically, you can find that in Hebrews 10:19–22, "Therefore, brothers and sisters, since we have the confidence to enter the Most Holy Place by the blood of Jesus...let us draw near to God with a sincere heart and with the full assurance that faith brings, having our hearts sprinkled to cleanse us from a guilty conscience and having our bodies washed with pure water." In other words, I have full assurance God wants me to come to Him.

This book speaks to taking our thoughts captive to the obedience of God, and after twenty-seven days, I can honestly tell you it is beginning to happen consistently. Before today, I did not realize how many negative thoughts I had. I also realize that these thoughts are accompanied by feelings. The thought that a class assignment could be difficult instantly came with feelings of defeat. Feelings and thoughts are two separate things and both can be given to God. As soon as that thought came in, a Scripture that battled that thought with the truth came also. With these thoughts, I was able to edify myself and glorify God.

This may sound similar to the post from the other day but that is the beauty of it. God is building on the foundation He is laying. I am growing and God is aligning me with the mind of Christ.

G ushy, that's what I feel. All I feel is love. The amount of revelation and insight God is giving me about people is incredible. Just last night I looked at a girl at a meeting I was in, and I knew she was looking to move out and move in with someone, because the rent was getting to be too high. In my own thinking I found this odd because I knew she has a good job and has been at her apartment for a while. Nevertheless, this morning, an e-mail was received stating that she was looking to rent a room in someone's home because her rent was being raised.

> No longer do I call you slaves, for the slave does not know what his master is doing; but I have called you friends, for all things that I have heard from My Father I have made known to you. (John 15:15)

I should have prayed for her but I did not realize that at the time. God is gracious and I am sure I will get another chance.

While doing the dishes and cleaning, suddenly I was overwhelmed with His presence. Joy came over me and I felt like dancing. Those that know me know I am very conservative and dancing is just not one of those things I do. Yet, I don't care anymore if it is for God. I do not know if I walk into His presence or His presence walks into me. Often times it is unexpected and truly wonderful. I lack the words to describe what it feels like. It is as if waves made up of the fruits of the Spirit hit me and I become undone; all I wanted to do is sing to Him and share every thought with Him while at the same time wanting to sit at His feet and listen to all He has to say. It is a sense of comfort and satisfaction that nothing or no one else can give.

The following are some other blessings that occurred during the course of the week that I did not journal.

- On a few occasions, people have spoken to me and as they are speaking, God is telling me exactly what is going to happen; sometimes the Holy Spirit tells me how the conversation is going to end and what they are going to ask me or sometimes the Holy Spirit shares things that will be happening to that person. For example, a friend came up to me and said she wanted to come over for coffee. I invited her for the next morning. She confirmed, but the Lord impressed upon me that she would not be able to make it and for a very specific reason. The next day she sent me a text message telling me she cannot come and her reason was the very reason God had shared.

- I started off strong in being conscious of God's presence at the very least once every half an hour, but I've slacked, not on purpose but I have nonetheless, yet God has not. He has met me every day.

Day 29

I woke up more than once from a deep sleep crying out in my thoughts to God saying, "I want to know You, Lord."

My spirit has been quickened, it has been made alive to the Word of God. Even as I sleep, my soul longs for a face-to-face encounter with the living Lord. I am yearning more for Him. I no longer just want to walk in the miraculous, instead I want Jesus. I want to know every facet of His glorious ways and walk in them. I have limited God, and it is time to take the limits off Him.

Day 30

The past few days I have been slacking as they say. I have not been as conscious of my time with God as far as purposely stopping what I am doing for a moment and fellowshipping with Him. This morning I woke up with the urge to dance and sing before the Lord again; it has not happened in a few days. It was glorious as His presence graced me with gold dust on my hand. As I worshipped, He reminded me of things that needed to be done without the stress that comes with having to do them; there was peace and joy that abounded. He reminded me of who I am in His eyes; royalty, a priesthood, and a beloved daughter. There is no sweeter feeling than knowing you are completely protected by the maker of the universe. Even if tribulations come, He is there by my side to help me through it.

Day 31

*A*s I gave thanks to God this morning for the things I tend to take for granted—a husband who blesses me and does not stand in the way of God's calling on my life, children who are healthy and happy, and a loving pastor who I love like a brother and honor as a father—I am humbled by God's kindness and His bigness in comparison to me. Not big in a bad way as God is not out to belittle us or humiliate us but in the sense of the protection I have as His child.

You may hear someone say to you, "Jesus loves you," then they walk away. Well, it is true, even if you have not accepted Him yet as Savior. There were two things I always prayed for as a child. One was to be able to go to church. I longed to have a priest/pastor like the ones on TV, one that would give me his personal number to reach him in case of emergency, one that was there for me just for counseling, one that would mentor me, and one that would teach me the Scripture and pray with me. Years passed, a whole lifetime one may say, but then at thirty-eight years old, God gave that to me through my current pastor. In him, I have a spiritual father, a spiritual big brother, and a friend. Then God went over and beyond and put two more pastors in my life who have a similar relationship with me. God went even beyond that and has allowed me to be that kind of person to other people.

The other thing I prayed about as a child was what my husband would be like. Every little girl I think dreams about these things. Seeing how my parents argued made me want very specific things in my husband. God provided everything I ever wanted in a husband and so much more. He has faults, many as do I, but every specific thing I had asked God for as a child/teen in a husband God has given me in my beloved Tony. All this to say that yes, God really does love you and hears your prayers.

As God has been opening my eyes to the blessings around me, I can't help but to want to go on my knees and say, "Thank you," to a loving God who has given His little girl the desires of her heart.

Today I experienced a moment of comforting that was unexpected and greatly needed. Sometimes people say careless things in passing without realizing the weight of their words. I was involved in a conversation where something was said jokingly and it was as if a dagger went through my heart. Instantly, I pictured the Father putting my head against His chest and comforting me. God helped me get through the rest of that conversation without falling apart.

Through this forty day experiment my understanding of God has changed. I do not have to pray, "Oh God help" out of desperation in a hurtful conversation. God is there comforting me before I even ask. This knowing that God is already there also affects the way the conversation can end. If I had not been aware of God's presence, I could have fallen captive to offense or unforgiveness. Perhaps I could have even said something hurtful to the other person. Knowing God was in the room allowed me to take my thought captives and not respond out of anger but out of love.

Day 32

Waking up feeling the Holy Spirit by your side was one of the best feelings. There was no stress as I thought about the day that was before me. There was joy and an energy that can only come from God. As I ministered in the church today, the Lord led me to say and share things that I had never done before in the ministry I was involved in; however, knowing it was God, I happily obeyed and saw this person who was receiving ministry receive freedom through Christ. On the way home I felt the Lord say to stop at a particular store. I must admit I ignored it the first time not realizing it was God. The second time I heard the Lord speak, I realized it was God and went right to that store. He told me where to park. As I turned off my vehicle, I happened to look out the side window and saw an older lady in her seventies fall. Due to the location of the fall and the position of her car, it was highly unlikely anyone would see her laying on the ground from the parking lot. Through Christ's leading, I was able to pray His words for her and see her experience great peace. Whenever I stopped praying, fear would overcome her and she would start shaking; when I prayed His words, she was instantly calmed down. This went on for about thirty minutes as we waited for the ambulance to take her away.

Day 33

*A*s I went about my morning routine, I found myself going over a possible conversation I may be having with my friend. No mention had been made of this conversation. The conversation may not even take place, yet I found a need to go over in my head every possible scenario and how I would respond. I had been on the defense with this person without even speaking to them. Within a few minutes, in my mind I had come up with what I would say if they said this or they said that. Within a minute, I could feel my body tensing up. I repented for stress and anxiety as they are just socially acceptable names for fear. Seconds later I found myself in the same cycle. Out of desperation, I asked the Lord for help. Ever so softly I heard, "Turn the concern into a prayer."

I believe the Lord just gave me one of the secrets to a stress-free life; pray it and leave it at the cross.

God speaks to me personally, but He also speaks to me through others, via prophetic words. Today at church service, someone spoke a prophetic word to me about finances. The word was specific. Without going into details, I was told to just believe. I went to the altar, repented of unbelief, and asked God to help me with my unbelief. That evening I received a call notifying me that someone donated a substantial amount toward a mission trip I would be going on next month. This amount combined with the donations I had received covered the exact amount of the trip plus the visa and other miscellaneous items that were required for this mission trip. God put a desire in my heart to go to the nations and He also is providing the way.

Day 34

*W*e as humans tend to choose what the flesh wants: what is easy, feels good, is convenient, benefits us, and brings us worldly happiness. Still, these things disappear. Only the things that God brings are eternal and can satisfy the soul. The flesh does not need to be satisfied, but God in His mercy sometimes does both. God will simultaneously allow us to have an eternal thing that also satisfies that fleshly desire because He loves us. Today was that day for me. Since childhood, I dreamed of "working for God," as I used to call it. As a Catholic girl, I thought my only option was to be a nun which I considered until I met my husband. I thought any shot of ever doing anything for God was gone. Obviously, there was a lot I did not know.

Today, I get to minister in different ministries at the church I attend and devote almost all of my time to kingdom things. One of the things I have wanted to do for many years now was to preach the gospel at a service and maybe one day baptize someone. Today at the nursing home I volunteer at my desires came to pass. It was only five people, but the Lord allowed me to preach the gospel. Then just like in the book of Acts, one person heard the gospel; her spirit was quickened and asked to be baptized. She was baptized immediately. Today a childhood desire was satisfied. I can suppose you can say my flesh was satisfied as a dream came true. After the service was over and I was cleaning up, the team I was with and I prayed a prayer of thanks to the Lord for what He had done. At that moment I felt the weight of His presence. I was overcome and wept. Why I wept, I don't know except all I could say is that the more I felt His presence, the more I wept. At that moment, my soul was satisfied. It was amazing. Never give up faith. Even a child's silly thoughts of "working for God," God can make come true.

Day 35

*F*ear is the opposite of faith. If we fear we are not having faith that God will come through for us. After yesterday's spiritual victory, I came home to one sick child and spent the day with the other one getting X-rays for a possible buckle fracture. As I sat at the hospital waiting for results, I kept thinking that this was the enemy attacking my kids. I could feel fear approaching as I thought, *If this is what happens when I baptize two people, what will happen when I become ordained?*

As quickly as that thought entered my mind, I heard the Lord say, "I will always protect her." Hearing the sweet voice of God gives me supernatural boldness to go out and preach the gospel; to me that is like giving the devil a punch right in the gut.

Day 36

I have heard it said that prayer is simply a conversation with God. I believe that, but if pressed, I must admit I thought of it as formal conversation. It starts with dear Lord, Papa, or in Jesus' name and ends in Amen. There is nothing wrong with praying this way. God is a holy God and must be respected and awed. When I converse with my friends, I don't start the conversation with dear Angie and finish it with an Amen. In fact, most of the time I may start off by just saying what's on my heart. If the friend is a really close friend, sometimes hellos and pleasantries are not necessary. I know that he or she will listen and comfort me. They know I love them and it is not my desire to be rude, but sometimes it happens. Why? It happens because I am self-absorbed in my own problems.

Feeling overwhelmed by the side effects of a condition I am dealing with, last night as I lay in bed, I simply said, "I'm having a tough time. I feel I cannot think straight."

I shared with God how inept I feel when this condition seems to take over. I specifically told God I was struggling with doing the small tasks at home—things like organizing my daughter's medication for the week seemed impossible. Tasks that should take minutes took me hours and were left unfinished. I told God how scattered my thoughts felt and how difficult it had been to start work on a class paper. I told Him I could not remember what I had finished or what needed to be done. Sometimes the day just flies by in confusion.

Afterwards, I drifted off to sleep. There was no Amen at the end of the prayer. I spoke to the Holy Spirit as if I were talking to my best friend; I spilled my guts to Him.

This morning I woke up and to my surprise, I cleaned the kitchen and organized my daughter's pills. I started to organize for an upcoming trip. Then I did some homework and made headway on the paper that I'm to be working on and other homework assignments. To my delight, I finished what I needed to do for class, baked dessert, made dinner, and spent time with the kids (school was closed due to snow). I have done more today than I have been able to do in a few days. Granted what I got done may not seem like much to the average person, but I am not your average person. I have a condition that sometimes debilitates me. (By His stripes I am healed but until my body catches up with Scripture things are sometimes difficult.) These little things that I was able to complete today were the specific things I had told God about before I went to bed.

As I reflect back on this day I realize that God is my friend. He is not a God that requires formalities all the time. He understands the human condition. I know that if I would have told my best friend, Barb, what I was going through, she would have done things to ease my day. Just like a best friend, Jesus did things to ease my day. He gave me the grace I needed to accomplish what I had to do that day and to edify me. Just as a husband does little things for his wife to let her know he loves her, so my Bridegroom did little things for me today to let me know He loves me.

Day 37

*A*s I lay in bed last night, for a few moments I was in complete bliss. For those moments, I had absolutely no worries and no problems. God died for my sins and saved me from an eternity in hell. On top of that, God is in me and with me forever—that was my only focus and it was wonderful. I slipped into a deep, peaceful sleep. Then morning came. I tried but could not get that feeling back. The more I tried, the worse things got. My husband was annoying, the dog was barking, the plumbing broke, and there was no hot water; you get the picture. Thinking I had something to do with the feeling I had last night in the first place and not realizing it was a grace from God, I decided to do something about it. I decided to worship. In my worship time, I was quickly convicted and grieved at how little faith I had. Half my day was spent trying to capture a feeling that was a gift from God and the other half of the day was spent repenting and feeling bad that I probably grieved the Holy Spirit.

I felt bad about my lack of faith and even angry at God for giving me that feeling of complete ecstasy for lack of a better word and then taking it away, then I felt bad for acting like a brat and being mad at God. I spent the day focusing on myself and not God. In almost twenty-four hours I went from one extreme to the other. When I finally realized that guilt is not of God and repented, I could feel the Holy Spirit holding me close to Him. He never stopped loving me despite my childish behavior.

Day 38

Throughout this experiment I've written a few times about God's desire to bless us—to bless us not just once but to bless us in intimate ways giving things that we may not deserve but deep down want. I was a recipient of such a gift. I will be going on a mission trip out of the country in March. The total of the trip including the visa which was not part of the price and several other things we needed to pay came close to four thousand dollars. God has provided the exact amount that I needed through people that donated the funds for me to go. I did not advertise I was going nor did I solicit money. I did, however, tell a few close friends to keep me in their prayers for this. What I am about to say next is where you really see God's heart for me (and for you too when you give Him your desires).

I had thought to myself it would be nice if I could cut my hair and dye it before I go. Would you believe if I totaled the donations I received, it was exactly enough for the trip plus the exact amount I need for the beauty parlor? God supplied everything, even my wants to the penny. Our God is a God that wants to see His kids happy and is excited to give us things.

Day 39

The Lord speaks to us as we have already established. When God speaks to us, it is for a reason that sometimes we may not know until we get to heaven, but even so, we should still listen. Regardless of whether the results are immediate or for a future time, we should always be obedient to the word from the Lord.

On Wednesday of this week I was going through my journal, and back in late October I wrote that I should go to a particular Christian conference that was going to be in Pennsylvania. I had forgotten about this conference. I considered it, the finances, and the travel time involved and had decided on not going. On Friday of this same week, I found a note on my desk dated late January, "Go to the conference." This was the second time God had told me to go to the conference. I decided to listen. My daughters and I went to the conference with our friends. The conference was in itself outstanding, but throughout it I saw how God did little things for me. It was a great bonding time with my kids. My girls and I got to spend lunch time with someone whom I love and respect dearly, and the friend that we rode with is just amazing. We got to share ideas about possible outreaches and had a great conversation all the way home.

I do want to mention one thing. There was one speaker at the conference who when he went up to speak my heart started pounding out of my chest; I thought for sure he was going to have a prophetic word for me or I was going to have an impartation or something.

Well, the speaker spoke and left and I got nothing. We were all up extremely early and exhausted; since we had a long drive ahead of us, we decided to leave before the conference ended that night. At first I was disappointed that I had not gotten a chance to speak or get prayer from any of the speakers. Nonetheless, when I realized my feelings I repented of them. It's okay to want to receive from someone with an anointing but no reason to be disappointed if he/she doesn't; after all it is God we follow not a person. It's easy to feel a little left out when everyone around you seems to be getting something you desire. After a prayer of repentance and thanksgiving, something really amazing happened. My friend was by the doors waiting for me. When I got there, she told me she told my daughter to speak to the one speaker that I had mentioned and then told me, "Go stand by her and get a word."

I stood by my daughter only because we were in the middle of the hallway and many were passing by. Sometimes when a Word of the Lord comes, you fall under the weight of His glory and the power of His word. I didn't want my daughter to receive a word from this prophet and not have anyone to catch her if she was going to fall.

She got her word and the prophet also gave me a word—one that was very personal and one that demonstrates that God hears our prayers. What this man said as a prophetic word that he sees the Lord doing in my life is something that I had been pressing in for. To me it was confirmation that God not only hears our prayers but whatever you say in Jesus's name will be given if aligned with His will. What this prophet said and what I had been praying for was specific and not your everyday kind of generic word that can be something to everyone.

Why the Lord had told me to go to this specific conference, I don't know. It could have been for all the reasons I mentioned above or it could have been because of what I received through global impartation. I will know for sure one day. If anything, however, it was worth going just to see God's attention to personal details in my life. God knew I was disappointed I did not get a chance to speak to that prophet, yet moments before I left I had a divine appointment with him. Within those five minutes I spent with the man of God, God not only gave me a desire of my heart but confirmed He hears me.

*T*oday the Lord gave me great insight on a particular Scripture verse that was a stumbling block for me because I could not see the verse being read in a tone of love. Funny thing about Scripture is that if you read it without the help of the Holy Spirit, you may only be reading words emptied of the love they are carrying. Remember Scripture is the Word of God and the Word was God. Therefore, all the Scriptures should be read under the lens of love, because God is love. After I finally understood this particular verse and the love behind it, I could feel the Holy Spirit come upon me; the weight of His presence was evident in that my husband who had no clue what had been revealed to me nor what I was feeling looked over and said, "What's going on with you?"

It was as if shackles were taken off me and the incredible peace of God just flooded every area of my body.

I challenge you to take your own 40 day challenge. I would love to hear how it goes and pray with you. You may email me at the40dayexperiment@gmail.com.

Over the past few weeks, I can honestly tell you my life has been changed for the better. There are things that we hear in our Christian walks that are nice to hear, but we believe they are for someone else. Even as believers we hear of God's goodness, and we may think it's for someone else. The one thing that I learned and cannot emphasize enough during this experience is that intimacy with God is a choice. To say "if God wants to be intimate with me, He will make it happen" is a cop out and another way of saying I do not want to put the effort in. Yes, God can do anything supernaturally, but still I believe it is our choice.

Experiencing the presence of God is a choice that turns into a lifestyle. Intimacy with God is more than just friendship; it is a deep knowing of one another, and this can be achieved by doing things together. Invite God into your everyday activities. Read the Bible to know the characteristics of God.

Dying to self is also a choice. Intimacy with God reveals the truth of sin. Sin is disgusting and revolting to God. We should desire to look at sin as God does and turn away from the sin, this is repentance. We must be willing to die to our pride, to our desires, and to anything that stands in the way of drawing near to God and be willing to submit to the Lordship of Christ Jesus, letting God have control of every part of us, sanctifying our bodies to God as a living sacrifice.

The fear of man, which is in very basic terms fear of being judged, made fun of, or ridiculed, hinders our intimacy with Christ. Fear of man is rooted in pride. Pride was Satan's downfall and the downfall of many in the Scriptures. Pride is subtle; you are usually the last one to know you have it yet everyone else sees it.

It does not matter what you believe right this second; I can tell you for sure that God loves you. God speaks right into the thing that troubles you the most. There is no double talk with God. It is all about faith. God does not care how many degrees you have, how many titles are before your name, or how many initials after it you have. There are many people who do not run a church, do not have doctorates, or have not even been ordained but they still pray and see miraculous things happen, why? The miraculous happens because their faith is in Jesus and not in their achievements.

God is kind. God will not put a dream in your heart to taunt you with it. If God has given you a desire, pray into it and press in; it will come to pass. Stay strong and steadfast, keeping your eyes on the kingdom; God will not forsake you. We have to give God a chance to work in our lives. God loves to give you little surprises that make your heart jump with joy.

Intimacy with Christ is not about a legalistic routine. We can choose to set apart a certain time of day to have our "quiet time with the Lord," but the truth is life happens and we can't always do what we plan. But God knows our hearts; if one day we spend three hours and the next few times we can only spend ten minutes with Him uninterrupted, that's okay too. The point is to honestly try.

Finally, I want to leave you with three thoughts:

- The battle is mostly in the mind. If our minds are fully captured or given to Jesus we overcome it all. We should not be worried by the tribulations we are in because we should be counting it all joy.

- Read the Bible first, then read the books about the Bible. Books about the Bible cannot pierce your heart the way the Word of God can. Do not let a man direct your actions or thinking; let it be God that renews your mind.

- Let your actions be for the sake of pleasing God alone. People will have an issue with that, but that is their problem. Obedience to God's Word has more value than pleasing men.

Conclusion

Some who have read this book right now may think that talking to God is weird. Others may think that hearing God is odd. Some may think that having a conversation, speaking to God, and hearing His response is not only crazy but impossible. Actually, it is not. Since the beginning of humanity, God has conversed with His children. In Genesis, we see Adam and God frequently conversing. It was the fall of man that made speaking to the Lord not a commonplace thing, but it is still available to us. Look at Romans 15:4, you will see that Scripture is given for instruction; we are supposed to commune with God. If anything, the ability to have conversations with God has been a treasure that has been lost or forgotten in some denominations. Now is the time to dig up that treasure, open the box, and enjoy all of its benefits! It is a free gift to every believer. Do not waste any more time wondering if God will speak to you or if you are worthy of such lofty things as a conversation with the Almighty Himself. The answer is *yes*! God wants to talk to you and He also wants to listen to you. You have value, and what you say is important to God. How do I know this if I have never met you, you may ask? Simple, Jesus died for you. If that is not giving you value, I don't know what else is.

Over the past forty days I have attempted to take every thought captive. Some days were more successful than others. Yet, through this process, as I drew near to God by renewing my mind with Bible verses and worship; God drew near to me. I started this experiment to prove that intimacy with God was possible for anybody. A key step towards intimacy is taking every thought captive to the obedience of Christ, what does that mean? It means renewing your mind with what God says about you and about the situations you may be in, thereby removing any lies you may be believing from Satan. As I began to renew my mind I realized just how much I am loved by God. It is human nature to love those that love us, the more I realized how much God loves me the more I wanted to love God back. How do we love God back? We love God back by giving of ourselves, loving the person in front of us, and giving all glory to God knowing that every good and perfect thing comes from God. The next step is realizing that the devil is real and he comes to steal, kill, and destroy but because of Jesus' sacrifice on the cross we now have authority over the devil and his demons. Walking in the power and authority Jesus died for us to have while giving Him the glory is another way to love God. The ways to love God are endless.

Another key to intimacy is worship. Worship God, tell God who He is to you. Thank Him for His goodness, thank God for all the blessings in your life. Then go one step further and thank God for the answer to your prayers (even before they are answered) and thank Him for making a way out for any bad situation you may be in. He is God Almighty and He is worthy to be praised.

Reading the Bible is an excellent way to become intimate with God. The Bible is God's Word and the Word is God. Reading Scripture will reveal to you what God thinks about you, His plans for you, all the aspects of who God is and so much more.

Although there is no one formula or cookie cutter way to achieve intimacy with Christ, I will share with you some practical practices. Please do not make this about works, everything that has happened to me is a grace from God. The things I did, I did out of love and admiration for my Savior. Here is a summary of some things that can also help you achieve a more intimate relationship with Christ.

- When you wake up give your day to God. Do this by listing all the things you have to do and asking God to be part of it and to guide you through it.

- Pray every morning that the works God has created for you to do since the beginning of time you may complete them in your lifetime.

- Specifically set aside time to spend in prayer, Scripture reading and worship (sometimes you may spend more time than planned for and others less due to circumstances but that is okay), it is about a willingness to say, "Yes".

- Take every opportunity you have to pray for others or give a prophetic word.

- Actively search for God in every situation in your day. Do this by asking God to show you something good about the situation. If the Holy Spirit is in you, then you are a carrier of His glory which means there is something of God wherever you go. You are bringing God's glory into the situation and that should be evident. Sometimes we have to look a bit harder than other times, but that's okay too,

- When you get the urge to pray or worship or sing to the Lord or even dance, do it. Be obedient to His gentle voice drawing you near to Him.

- When you get the urge to contact someone out of nowhere, do it. It is probably the Holy Spirit prompting you to be there for that person in some way.

- Try the "one-minute test."

- Read the Bible.

- Fast.

- Listen to worship music.

- Give thanks in all things.

- Do everything as if you were doing it for God Himself.

- Go to church.

- In between church services, listen to online biblically sound sermons to keep your spirit nourished during the week.

- Rest in God.

- If you have a prayer language, then speak it, every day, throughout the day.

- Be joyful. Happiness is dependent on circumstance, but joy comes from within. If you cannot find anything to be joyful for then rejoice in the fact that Jesus died for your sin and took your penalty at the cross. If you have accepted Jesus as Savior, you will not burn in hell for eternity. That's a good reason to rejoice, don't you think?

These are just a few suggestions that I incorporated into these last forty days that have helped me achieve a greater intimacy with Christ.

The following is a list of what has occurred in my life because of this forty-day experiment:

- I have been able to hear God's voice clearly and accurately.

- My spiritual gifts have been sharpened.

- I am more aware of the Holy Spirit's presence in my every-day tasks.

- My love for God has become deeper.

- I now can read the Bible for extended periods of time while receiving revelation from the Lord.

- I am no longer shy about worshiping in front of others in small group settings.

- I have learned how to quickly recognize a bad thought and quickly replace it with a godly one.

- I now can worship and praise God for hours and be completely lost in his presence.

- I recognize the Holy Spirit's presence, I am beginning to understand the ways of God when it comes to how He communicates with me.

- The fact that I have remained peaceful in times where in the past I may not have has affected my kids and husband in a positive way, now everyone is peaceful no one is on "flight or fly" mode anymore.

- My confidence has skyrocketed, not in myself but in God. I can trust that what the Holy Spirit says is correct.

- My faith has increased.

- I will never have to wonder again if God hears me.

There are many more benefits that I can share with you about this forty-day experiment that have forever changed me, but my intent is to whet your appetite. I invite you to do your own forty-day challenge it will change your life. Your 40 day experiment will turn into a lifestyle of intimacy with God. As I mentioned earlier, feel free to email me as to how it's going at the40dayexperiment@gmail.com. I will encourage you and pray for you.

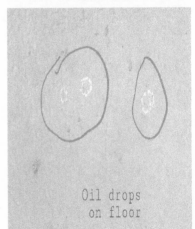

About the Author

Barbara Colacchia is a faith-filled individual who believes that God is the same yesterday, today and forever. Through the Holy Spirit that Christ has filled her with, she has been able to serve others through prayer and has seen may miracles such as: legs grown, paralyzed limbs move, driven a car with a dead battery for over a week and fixed appliances simply by praying over them in Jesus' name, and seen many healed. Barbara is the mother of two daughters and has been faithfully married for over twenty years.

CPSIA information can be obtained
at www.ICGtesting.com
Printed in the USA
BVHW071121070119
537203BV00007B/927/P

9 781644 165607